VIGNETTES

FROM *My French Village*

VIGNETTES

FROM *My French Village*

Dayle
DOROSHOW

proving
press

Book Design & Production:
Columbus Publishing Lab
www.ColumbusPublishingLab.com

Copyright © 2022 by
Dayle Doroshow
LCCN: 2022918878

Hardback ISBN: 978-1-63337-681-6
Paperback ISBN: 978-1-63337-682-3
E-Book ISBN: 978-1-63337-683-0

Printed in the United States of America
1 3 5 7 9 10 8 6 4 2

MANY THANKS, MERCI BEAUCOUP! to all my French friends, my family, all the lovely people who came to La Cascade, my Dan, and to the village of Durfort, who welcomed us from the beginning with open arms.

Table of Contents

1.
The Discovery

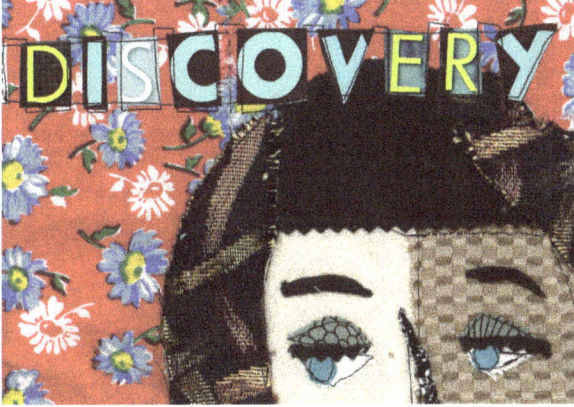

Textile art by Dayle

MY REAL LIFE IN FRANCE BEGAN IN 2003. My dream life of France began many years before when airline tickets from New York City to Paris were a mere ninety-nine dollars. In 1985 I had an opportunity to stay with a friend in a teeny hamlet (only five farmhouses) in the Dordogne region of France for three weeks with no car. We took walks, chatted with neighbors (in atrocious French), picked berries to make our own jam, gathered fresh eggs from the chickens, harvested garden veggies right outside our door, got milk and bread from a little putt-putt truck that came twice a week, and made bountiful flower arrangements and gourmet meals from the garden. This was the beginning of my love affair and dream of living in France one day. Come along with me as our journey begins.

LE RETOUR– RETURNING

I yearn to return to our little village in south-west France, even though I know there might be problems that await us on arrival. Perhaps the water heater will not click on, and I'll have to suck it up and get a cold shower after twenty-six hours of traveling. Or the car battery, which our friend has been taking care of over the last several months, will not turn over, and

Our village street

we won't be able to get to our favorite grocery store (always the first thing we look forward to!) After seventeen years of making this yearly journey, this sweet village has become our second home.

Usually, upon arriving at the Toulouse airport we hop the airport shuttle bus into Centre Ville and get on the local bus that takes us to Revel, the larger town five minutes from our tiny village. This bus trip takes about an hour; the bus rocks softly from side to side, and it's easy to be lulled asleep. I try to stay awake, as I want to see the beautiful rolling countryside of green meadows and golden hay fields. The ancient villages we pass through are framed by high Pyrenees mountains in the distance. This year, though, our lovely neighbor insists on picking us up at the airport. "You have traveled for many, many hours," she said. *"Non!* Not the bus. I will pick you up." She even drives us to a little grocery store so I can get coffee, bread, and wild cherry jam for the morning.

As soon as we arrive we hear welcoming and jolly hellos from neighbors out in the street. *Mesdames* Collette and Yvette, two of the older residents who have lived here for over fifty years; Olivier and Florence, who share their beautiful home with their daughter and her daughter, five-year-old Alice; our neighbors across from us, Eric and Sandrine, hang out their second-story window to welcome us back. *"Le retour?"* they all ask. We have returned? And for how long?

Our village is very human scale; the houses touch each other but are separated by three-foot-thick stone walls, so each house is very quiet. The shutters and flower boxes are a riot of colors; our shutters are a lovely Provençal blue. An important part of life in a small friendly French village is social relationships. Sometimes walking up the street to the house is an experience in international relations. In our village, Durfort (approximately two hundred people), we have older French people who are living in the houses in which they were born, young French families who have brought lots of energy to the village, and Moroccan, German, British, Irish, Dutch, and three Americans. We non-natives all have in common our bad French! But armed with a smile and a willingness to connect, we have a grand journey in communication, filled with lots of laughter.

THE DISCOVERY

How did we find this precious village that has become our home? France has been a love of mine since first flying from NYC to Paris in the 1980s for ninety-nine dollars. In 2003, after almost twenty years, my husband Dan and I returned to southern France. We drove down a long road to a small village nestled against the *Montagne Noire,* the Black Mountain—a tiny hamlet of three charming streets,

Gwen Gibson

a small church, and Café le Cyrano on the village square—all surrounded by the sounds of water. The River Sor cascades on one side of the village, a river that once had thirteen working textile and copperware mills. On the other side, running down the center of each of the three streets, are small trickling waterways left from the medieval days of quenching hot copper pots—now the perfect spot to chill a bottle of wine. The earth-colored cobblestones at the bottom glisten as the water runs over them. We were charmed by the village from the moment we arrived, but we had no idea at that time that we would find a future here. My heart immediately fell hard for this village.

We came to see an extraordinary friend, Gwen Gibson, who had recently bought an old village house from 1680 with three credit cards! Gwen was one of my first jewelry teachers and lived in the San Francisco Bay Area, so I saw her now and then at classes and conferences. In 2001, I had heard through the grapevine that she had bought a house in France and spent a year and a half renovating it into an artist's workshop home. I wrote her a short note congratulating her on this new adventure and mentioning that, one, I had loved France for years, and two, I could paint, sew, drill, etc., and was willing and wanting to help her on this house in any way possible in exchange for a bed to sleep in.

When I ended up in Europe in 2003 with an extra week by myself and nowhere to go, I contacted Gwen and asked if I could stay with her and help renovate La Cascade, so named for the free-falling waterfall outside the back of the house. She said *Oui!* By the time I arrived the hard renovation had been done, and what was left to do was furnish the house, sew curtains and pillows, hang lamps, and other decorative projects.

That week with Gwen was one of the highlights of my life. We spent a week sewing, going to the hardware store, shopping at Ikea (Yes! There is one in Toulouse!) for kitchen, studio, and bedding goods, the Moroccan store in Revel for gorgeous handwoven rugs and pillows, and the thrift stores and flea markets for beautiful old furnishings. It was a shock to see that gorgeous antique armoires only cost fifty euros or so! And the *chevettes* with marble tops (nightstands), fifteen euros. The secondhand stores are packed with these beauties from the 1800s to early 1900s, and the four bedrooms now all looked like they stepped right out of a French country magazine. We worked very hard but always with so much laughter and fun.

At night we were too tired to cook, so dinner was a buffet on the new kitchen island from Ikea. A loaf of bread, a dish of olive oil, a dish of balsamic vinegar, and a plate of confit tomatoes. Slap a slice of bread down into the olive oil, then into the vinegar, then top with a tomato, and pop into the mouth. Divine!

At the end of the week our friendship had deepened, and Gwen asked me to co-teach the first summer of classes at La Cascade in 2004. The studio on the third floor was not yet renovated—in fact, the third floor was a giant hole! So our studio in 2004 was in the *salon*, the living room. Six adventurous ladies took a leap of faith and joined us that summer. We worked with polymer clay and silk, making jewelry and handprinted soft silk purses. Each night at dinner one of us told a personal story of our ancestry or our art life or family life. That class was a joy. We all bonded closely, and it was a very special beginning to the magic of La Cascade and Gwen. This was a dream come true and has been the most special time in my life for the last seventeen years.

HUNTING FOR A HOUSE

I was possessed. Definitely possessed. From the moment I saw the village and La Cascade, I wanted a little place of my own in the area. For four years, armed with an intrepid spirit and bad French, I set off to *les immobliers* (the real estate offices) to look for a house.

Our budget was extremely low, and the prices at this time were extremely high. One year I saw a small "cottage" in the window that was in our price range. The pictures were charming. I went into the office and with my bad French asked to see the house. The agent looked shocked, saying, *"C'est très, très petit,"* over and over again. That didn't matter to me. It was affordable!

Dan (who also looked shocked) and I traipsed off with the agent to where a remote dirt road ended in a large brushy field. We

Cottage at Moulin du Chapitre

plowed through the waist-high weeds, the agent in high heels and a tight skirt, and eventually came to a vineyard. Beautiful! I spied a small cottage a bit ahead—that must be it! And in the middle of a beautiful vineyard? I was enchanted!

We arrived at the cottage, which now seemed more like a rustic hut from another century. But I was still not discouraged. Dan, now in a cold sweat of horror, looked around and started to ask questions. Plumbing? Non. Electricity? Non. Can we build out? Non. Can we build up? Non. The house must stay exactly as it is. Plumbing and electricity would be very expensive to add. My hopes were dashed. I slunk back through the field to the car feeling absolutely discouraged.

In my journal that sad day, after four years on the house hunt, I wrote, *La reve est mort.* The dream is dead.

OUR FAUX FRENCH HOME: MOULIN DU CHAPITRE

Our dear friends Veronique and Bernard own a charming bed and breakfast, Moulin du Chapitre, two minutes away from La Cascade.

Vero is a vibrant earth
mother, a creative thinker
in all ways. Her curly red
hair is always (somewhat)
tamed with a bright colorful scarf. Dangling earrings
and a multicolored beaded
eyeglass chain with wild
glasses complete her outfit
for the day. It might be a

Vero the Hatmaker

lime green, hot pink, or bright orange ensemble—color should
be her middle name! Vero makes haute couture hats from recycled materials and travels from festival to festival in France and
other countries making them for the public. Bernard runs the
B&B, makes beautiful breakfast jams and other delights, and is
an accomplished actor. Since 2004, Dan and I have always stayed
there for a couple of nights each year.

One day I noticed a small cottage on their property. "What's
that?" I asked.

"Oh," said Vero, with a naughty smile. "It's a place for lovers!"

"Let me see it," I said, smiling too.

A sweet front porch surrounded by rose bushes welcomed
us, and there on the porch was a Moroccan tile table big enough
for me to host a dinner party for friends, something I had wanted
to do for so long. Inside on the ground floor was a combination
kitchen, dining room, and sitting room. The kitchen had everything we would need: stove and oven, small fridge, dishes, pots,
and pans. Comfy chairs were placed by the back window looking
out over the soothing River Sor. Upstairs was a loft bedroom—tall

enough to stand in, with an antique French armoire to hold all our belongings and a large table on which to write or do art. I felt a rush of excitement and joy. It was perfect for my pretend French house! And it was available for weekly rentals. I told Dan about it and he was as enamored of it as I was, so we began to stay here for two weeks after my workshops finished at La Cascade. It became my faux French home after I gave up my dream of owning a house in France in 2007. My dream was alive, just in a new variation.

A HOUSE FINDS US

I was done with house hunting and was enjoying my pretend house at Moulin du Chapitre. During my 2009 La Cascade art workshop, a participant told me she had spied a house for sale on the river side of our street. I was not interested,

Day one at our house

but I did offer to go with her and give an opinion, as I had seen so many houses over the years. There were things I could advise on, like ventilation, good light, how much renovation was needed, and price.

We met Martine, the real estate agent, and I noticed two things. The house was very interesting, with lots of potential even though it was a disastrous mess. There was a large garden that went down to the River Sor and a large garage attached to the side of the house—almost unheard of in this small village. Second, the prices not only had fallen a lot since the 2008 financial crisis, but Martine said, "Make an offer. The seller really wants to sell." Hmm…I thought, what does that mean in France?

The workshop ended and my student went home with a pipedream. Dan and I moved to a campground for our final ten days in France. I couldn't stop thinking about the house.

I told Dan how interesting the house was, and for the first time, he was intrigued. A couple days later we arranged to see the house together. I was already dreaming of how I would paint, hang artwork, fill the house with flea market treasures, plant a vegetable garden and a climbing rose bush to frame the original front door from the 1500s—you can see where my artist brain was at. But Dan asked all the practical questions to do with plumbing, electricity, etc. We also didn't have the money for the asking price, but once again Martine told us to make an offer.

We went back to our campsite and little tent for the weekend and to talk. Dan and I asked each other, what does that mean here in France—"make an offer"?

Three days later we met in Martine's office. Dan and I had settled on an offer below the asking price. Plus, since we did not know how offer/counteroffer negotiations worked in France, we decided to offer five thousand euros less than we could afford. Our conversation (originally in French) went like this:

Martine said, "So…"

"We really like the house," Dan said.

"Aaaand?"

"We would like to offer—" Here Dan gave our low price. I felt a bit embarrassed.

Martine turned away with a slightly disgusted look on her face but also with a calculator. We looked in alarm to the English translator, who said, "Be calm, be calm. She is calculating."

Martine turned to us and said, "If you will come up one thousand euros, then okay."

Dan and I side-glanced at each other, a bit in shock, as we were prepared to come up five thousand euros. "Okay," we softly said. Big Long Pause.

I said, "Now what happens? You must contact the seller, and back and forth and back and forth. We are camping and only here for a few more days!"

"Oh, I'll call him right now," Martine said.

Blah, blah, blah—Martine and the seller of the house spoke in rapid French, none of which we understood. Martine hung up and then said, "The seller says okay to your price!"

Dan and I looked at each other in disbelief and joy. We took a big breath and a big leap of faith. Nine months later, we were the proud owners of a fixer-upper from the 1500s. My dream came true!

A PLUMBER SAVES THE FIRST DAY

One of the weird things about buying our house was that we were not able to check if the electricity and plumbing actually worked. This was a bit disturbing, as the house is from the 1500s and had sat empty for several years. There had been some renovations done for a renter many years ago, but still, it had sat empty for a long time. But since there were no current electric or water accounts set up, we could not check until after the sale was done.

The first day we turned on the water it poured out from under our shower and down a small hole in the floor, which was right over the electric panel down in the garage. Yikes! A moment of panic and we quickly switched off the water. Now we needed a plumber.

We called our friend Ann. "Oh, I have a favorite plumber! Here is his number," she replied.

After three days of trying to reach him to no avail, we called another friend. "Oh," she said, "I have a favorite plumber! I will call him for you."

A day later, our friend Monique appeared on our street with a very large man towering over her. I was watering flowers with Ann, who looked up and said, "That's my favorite plumber, Akba!" (He seems to be everyone's favorite plumber.) Monique introduced us and in we went.

Akba went upstairs to look at the problem with curious Dan following close by. Akba said in French (well, we thought he said), "I'm going out to my truck to get a part." We nodded in agreement. Then we waited and waited and waited. Finally we accepted that we did not understand what he said in French. So, what did he say?

Four hours later Akba knocked on our door and headed back up to the bathroom, with curious Dan following close by, and within minutes the shower was fixed! Now it was time to pay. Monique had told us that we must pay in cash and that the estimate was 350 euros. Dan had that ready in his pocket, waiting for Akba to ask for it.

In halting English, Akba said, "You live in California, ooohhhh I love California. 'California Dreamin',' my favorite song."

In bad French, we said, "Where are you from, Akba?"

"Morocco," he replied. We had a short conversation about our dream to go to Morocco one day.

Dan finally asked, "What is the total to pay?"

"Oh, just one hundred euros," Akba replied.

And so our plumbing problem was solved, and we gained not only a wonderful plumber but a new friend.

THE MYSTERIOUS SHUTTER ETIQUETTE

First thing on arrival at our village in 2018, I spent the afternoon putting a new coat of Provençal blue paint on our shutters and garage door. They looked so worn when we drove up to our house that I was embarrassed. Our street is one of the most beautiful in the village. The houses have brightly colored shutters among the traditional grays, browns, and whites. Two of our neighbors have a lovely soft green, another further down the street is merlot red, another is a light turquoise blue, and my favorite is eggplant purple. Gorgeous. These colorful shutters, combined with flower boxes and large pots overflowing with zinnias, geraniums, and petunias, make for a tapestry of dazzling color. Climbing roses and healthy grapevines framing doors and windows complete the picture. I wanted our house to look

Our house, now with painted shutters

as good as possible, so shutter maintenance and planting the window boxes were high on my to-do list.

The French have a whole system in place for the opening and closing of shutters. According to our older neighbors, the shutters are closed all day so the thick stone walls can keep the house cool in the summer and warm in the winter. The shutters are opened late evening in the summer to let a cool breeze in overnight, then closed up again by midmorning the next day. In the winter cold, the shutters are kept shut most of the time. It's a daily, time-consuming routine for many residents. I understand the logic of it, but I don't want to be in a dark house all day and all night! I want the beautiful light that streams in from our garden and the view of the River Sor rushing by. So we just let it be what it will be. *Que será, será.*

HOW TO FURNISH A HOUSE WITH LITTLE MONEY: EMMAUS AND THE VIDE GRENIERS

Emmaus is a charitable movement founded in France by Priest Abbé Pierre in 1949 to combat poverty and homelessness. Their mission is to help people regain hope for the future, and they have thrift stores in France where we found the treasures that inexpensively furnished our house.

We often go to the Emmaus shop in Castelnaudary twenty-five minutes away. It is a treasure trove of secondhand furniture, knick-knacks, kitchen equipment, dishes galore, records, books, clothes, electrical goods, and French antiques. The prices are amazing. We purchased a beautiful rug for our guest room, a lovely antique dining room buffet, the large armoires for our bedroom and guest room, and most recently an antique stained-glass-paned wine cabinet, each for under fifty euros. The money goes to help provide housing, employment, and financial aid to those in need. As an

The flea market at Lautrec village

added benefit, they do deliver and will take any donations you have. Wandering through the aisles on a Saturday morning is almost as fun as going to the countryside flea markets.

AND THE VIDE GRENIERS

Sunday, during my art workshops at La Cascade (and every other Sunday, to be honest) is a day for exploring the French flea markets. It's also a delightful way to discover and explore new villages. Most towns have at least one annual flea market. Anyone who lives in the village is given a free space to show their wares. If there are empty spaces, then professional antique dealers can rent those spaces. On any given Sunday in the spring, summer, and fall, we can find two to three flea markets within a forty-five-minute radius of our village.

In France, these markets are called *vide greniers,* which literally means "empty the attic." And that is exactly what they are. You'll find antique treasures, children's toys, old and new postcards, records and books, clothes, farm tools, rusty keys and locks, beautiful dishes, gorgeous white linen tablecloths, antique buttons, silver jewelry, and furniture. It's endless. In our part of France, wonderful treasures can still be found at incredibly low prices, literally from ten *centimes* (cents) on up. The Paris flea markets are, of course, amazing, but I think our country flea markets have the best bargains. I never spend more than twenty euros and come back home with treasures for our house, as well as additions to my summer wardrobe. There are also ladies selling homemade jams and chutneys from their gardens and always a booth with delish sausages and *frites* (french fries).

Every year our village of Durfort has their vide grenier. Last year over seven thousand people attended, and there were treasures galore. I picked up a beautiful glass water pitcher in the shape of a cluster of grapes, a black-and-white vase from Turkey, fashion magazines from the 1920s, and a set of twelve yellow-and-white plaid china teacups and saucers—all for under four euros. These beautiful antique treasures had been sitting in someone's attic or cupboards for decades! Each year I like to focus on hunting for a particular item. One year it was antique buttons; one year, old linens; one year, antique metal parts— keys, drawer pulls, ancient locks, and all kinds of brass and silver goodies. Most recently, vintage perfume bottles to add to my niece's collection. You can't find a better way to treasure hunt and discover *La Belle France*.

THANK YOU TO OUR VILLAGE

It was the end of our first summer owning our 1500s fixer-upper. Dan had spent all summer cleaning up twenty years of grime and installing a toilet, fridge, stove, and other necessities like beds to make the house livable as we continued to work on it. Since I was working full-time at La Cascade, I wasn't there during the day to help. Many times he stood outside the front door trying to figure out how to get something large and heavy inside. We had not yet made many friends in the village, but time after time a neighbor, or even someone in the village that we

End of summer dinner

hadn't yet met, offered to help Dan with whatever chore was at hand.

Shortly before we returned to the States, we wanted to have a thank you dinner for all who had gone out of their way to help us over the summer. As we made the list, we soon saw that over fifty people in our tiny village of two hundred had reached out to help and make us feel welcome! I thought, oh my gosh, I can't do a dinner for fifty-plus! We decided to do an *apéro* for thirty-five and a sit-down dinner for nineteen.

An apéro—short for aperitif—is a relaxing get together, usually between 6:00 and 8:00 p.m., for wine and nibbles. It's a time to socialize and have a snack, but not ruin dinner.

At our garden apéro, Dan and I served all colors of wine—red, white, and rosé—along with fruit juices and Perrier for those who did not want alcohol. Our "nibbles" spread included nuts, crackers, olives, slices of Spanish chorizo, tiny cubes of goat and feta cheese (available at the grocery store already marinated), and squares of rose garlic tart. We were so pleased to welcome our new neighbors: Jackie and Kathy, with their two huge bull dogs; Roger, bearing a gift of a huge orange flowering plant bigger than himself; our Dutch neighbors along with their friends visiting from Spain; and many other neighbors and new friends.

The next night was our dinner for nineteen special friends. Dan grilled veggies on our ancient smoky barbecue, which had probably not been used in twenty years. I made chicken with fig and porto sauce, rice, and a garden salad with my favorite roasted shallot dressing. We had an amazing evening with old and new friends: Gwen, Jerry, and Nese, owners and chef at La Cascade; Vero and Bernard from Moulin du Chapitre; Antoine and Severine, our first French friends in the village; Ann and Peter from Great Britain; Remi from the Netherlands; Suzie and Janos from Germany; and others. We partied far into the night. What a wonderful way to start our home life in France!

RECIPES

TOMATOES CONFIT WITH HONEY AND THYME
Preheat the oven to 300°F. Cover a sheet pan with foil. Cut 2 lb. of tomatoes—different kinds if you like—into ¼-inch rounds and put into a bowl. I like to use cocktail tomatoes and cut them in

half horizontally. Mix together 2 Tbsp. olive oil, 2 tsp. honey, and ½ tsp. fresh lemon thyme. Pour over tomatoes and toss. Arrange the tomatoes on the sheet pan and bake for 1 hour until the tomatoes are soft and caramelized.

Rose Garlic Tart from the Village of Lautrec

Well…. I don't make my own pastry shells. So in France they have beautiful tart pastry ready-made at grocery stores, and in the USA I use puff pastry sheets or a deep-dish pie crust.

Mix together ¼ cup soft butter, 7 garlic cloves minced, and ½ cup parmesan cheese till it is a smooth paste. Add in ¾ cup pine nuts. In another bowl beat 4 eggs with ¾ cup crème fraiche and a bit of salt and pepper. Spread the garlic mixture on the bottom of the pastry shell. Cover with the egg mixture. Bake at 400°F for 45 minutes. Serve hot.

My Fave Roasted Shallot Vinaigrette

Preheat oven to 400°F. Peel and chop 3 shallots and 1 garlic clove. Spread in a small baking dish along with ½ cup olive oil. Roast for approximately 20 minutes until shallots are soft and caramelized. Drain this oil into a measuring cup and add extra olive oil to measure ⅔ cup. Place shallots, 1 sprig rosemary, and the olive oil into your salad dressing container. Add ⅓ cup white balsamic vinegar. Add 1 Tbsp. honey. Salt and pepper. Shake shake shake.

Fig and Manchego Chicken with Porto Sauce

Butterfly 4 chicken breasts so they open like a book. Cover them with plastic wrap and pound flat till they are about ½ inch thick. Spread 1 Tbsp. fig jam on each breast. Cover jam with 1 ½ Tbsp.

Manchego cheese. Roll up the chicken and secure with tooth-picks. Season chicken with salt and pepper. Heat 1 ½ Tbsp. olive oil in a skillet. Add chicken and brown on each side until chicken is done. Remove chicken. Add 1 minced garlic clove to the olive oil, along with ⅓ cup white port (or liqueur of your choice), and cook for 3 minutes. Then add ½ cup chicken stock, 1 tsp. Dijon mustard, and ½ cup heavy cream. Bring to a boil for 5 minutes, and cook till slightly thickened. Add chicken back in and coat with sauce.

2.
Settling into Village Life

Bakery delights

THERE'S ALWAYS A BIT OF TREPIDATION going from our home in the United States to France. These days, travel can be long and complicated. It helps to remind myself that it is a transition day, which will be over soon, and then I will be home again in France. And it is a home—not just a house. I've found that having a routine for the first few days really helps me settle in. It's a routine tried and true and one that I actually love.

DAY ONE

First morning after our arrival day in France is always special. I wake up with the sun and can hardly wait for the day to begin. Dan got the battery working in the car so we could get to the grocery store—one of our favorite first things to do. I pulled the things out of the armoires that I had put away when we left last year. It's such a pleasure to set out all my flea market treasures.

The car is working (hooray), and off we go to Revel—the larger town five minutes from us. Revel has one of the best Saturday regional markets—it is named one of the 100 Most Beautiful Markets in France. More on that later!

In Revel we get our car insurance for the five months we are here. Having car insurance is legally very important in France so it is always first on our list. Then on to Lidl—our favorite grocery store. Every week at Lidl a region of France or another country is featured via an array of specialty food items. This week is *Asie*, Asia. I stock up on coconut milk, tandoori flavored chips, sesame oil, different sauces, samosas, wasabi almonds, and lots of other goodies for apéros and dinners with friends.

Since we're in an Asian frame of mind we decided to treat ourselves to a Chinese buffet lunch—we have a good restaurant right here in Revel. I love the salad with thinly sliced chicken and a creamy honey-mustard dressing. I like to try a bit of everything—*nems* (spring rolls), fried calamari, and other assorted small dishes. For the main dishes, they offer chicken curry, tandoori chicken on a skewer, sweet and sour pork, beef and broccoli, sautéed shrimp with veggies, fried rice, and amazingly, Dan's favorite, fried frog legs! There is an assortment of desserts—Western and Asian—and a whole freezer of ice cream. Not to mention the chocolate fountain. All this for eleven euros, with seconds on anything—who can resist! After running our first-day errands, we're well fed, well stocked in the kitchen, and we're ready to begin another five-month adventure.

MY MORNING ROUTINE

First, a cup of good strong coffee. We have a French press here, and I've gotten in the delicious habit of adding a tablespoon of chocolate powder to my coffee. Poulain is my favorite—established in 1893, Poulain is one of the oldest chocolate makers in France.

I like to get up early and have half an hour to myself in our sweet kitchen. On our kitchen table are my French food magazines. This is one of

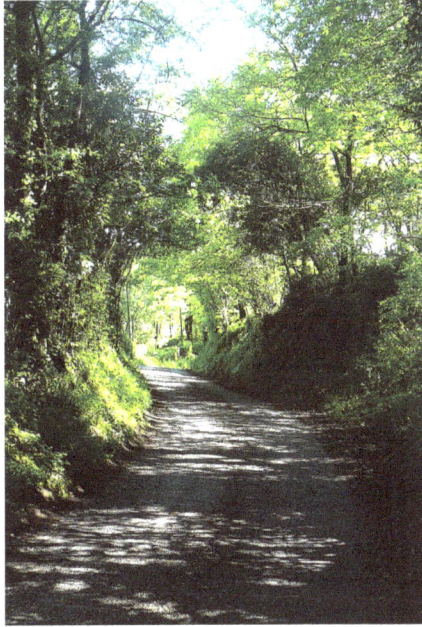

Early morning walk

several ways I'm learning French. The food mags provide many new nouns and verbs—*pavot* (poppy seeds), *bouillir* (to boil). Yep, all food-related, but still new words! Soon I'll break open a baguette or slice a piece of walnut bread to top with sweet butter and *confiture* (jam). I like the Bonne Maman mirabelle jam. Mirabelles are small bright yellow plums, sweet and full of flavor, and only available in late summer and early fall. Eaten fresh, in jam, in fruit tarts, and even liqueurs, they are a delight.

After fueling myself, I'm off for a walk. Each morning—well most of them—I do an exercise walk. Unbeknownst to me, I recently found out that I am known in the village as *L'Americaine Sportif* (the Athletic American). My fellow villagers see me out pumping my arms vigorously on my speed walk and assume that I am sporty. Ha! Hardly!

I have two main routes. One is up the mountain road that goes out the back end of the village. Our village nestles right up against the beautiful Montagne Noire (the Black Mountain). The road eventually ends at a higher village called Les Cammazes. The River Sor and the early morning birds provide a beautiful musical accompaniment to my walk. Along the road there are several abandoned old mills, which were the copper *ateliers* (studios) from the Middle Ages. The old weathered mill stones have been set out against the ivy and wisteria-covered stone buildings. Every so often there are gorgeous houses, one with a large uphill meadow with five horses grazing or rambunctiously playing with each other. Sometimes the horses come down to the gate for bread. It's a good use of the stale baguettes that can pile up in our kitchen. As I approach the gate, they sprint down to meet me and are ready for their morning treat.

I walk about forty-five minutes up, navigating the gentle switchbacks with the river waterfalls cascading on one side along with wildflowers, purple wisteria, wild raspberries, cherry, fig, and almond trees, chickens, horses, and who knows what else! Last Sunday I ran into two goats lazily meandering down the road and moments later twenty-two antique cars with drivers and passengers all decked out in 1920s garb, waving enthusiastically as I trudged up the mountain.

My second favorite walk is to the *boulangerie* in the neighboring village of Soreze. This walk takes fifty to sixty minutes depending on how fast I go. It starts in our village and the first five minutes is quite a steep uphill climb along the road called *Le Haute Chemin* (the High Road). This gravel and dirt path connects our village, Durfort, to Soreze. It's a beautiful walk—you have an overview of the green and gold rolling hills and the scattered terracotta-tiled-roof villages below us. I enter the outskirts of Soreze and continue to my destination—the bakery! I have been going to this bakery for years so now they greet me when I enter, *"Bonjour Madam,* What would you like today?" There is a wood-fired oven in the back and beautiful tempting desserts in addition to the wonderful breads and *patisseries.* Their *pain au noix* (walnut bread) is the best I have found. Second favorite is the *pain aux figues* (fig bread). The *croissants, pain aux raisins* (raisin rolls), and *pain au chocolat* are also delectable. As I hike back to Durfort, I tell myself that the walk itself justifies and balances out the partaking of these goodies—yes?

UNDER COVER OF DARKNESS

An added benefit of my early morning walks is watching several trees along the riverside bear fruit. There are two trees this year beckoning to me. In May as I approach house number four, there it is. My—well, not really *my*—cherry tree is full of drippy, juicy readiness. The cherries are bursting off the branches. I have been picking cherries from this tree under cover of darkness at 6:30 a.m. for the last two years. I feel a little guilty about the thievery, as there are cars parked at the house. On the other hand, I have never seen anyone here, and no one else besides the birds seems to be interested in the fruit. So they are mine, all mine! I get out my little plastic bag and fill it to the brim with cherries. I found a recipe in a French medieval cookbook that I'll try my hand at when I get back. Sounds like a cherry ginger scone from what I can translate. I'll let you know. And I'll make a batch of fresh cherry jam.

Now, September, it is fig season here in this part of France. There have not been many figs in the Revel market this year, so it is a huge surprise to see that this tree on my morning walk is full of beautiful figs. They are ripe and dropping to the ground. The owners of this house do not seem to be picking them either. I pick a couple each morning that are absolute perfection, ready to be eaten for breakfast, made into a fresh fig tart, or simply served with baked brie and bread—YUM. Who could ask for a more delectable exercise walk!

MY DAILY DRAWING

I have a commitment in France to do a daily drawing in my small journal. This is the one art practice I never miss. There are a few rules I set in stone. One, it's the first thing I do in the morning, along with my morning coffee. Whether it's at 5:00 a.m. or 8:00 a.m., it's the first thing I do. Two, I don't take longer than ten minutes per drawing. Three, I always use black ink: a Pentel fine point. No time or opportunity to

Fashion drawing with fabric

become angsty about the drawing, change, or erase it! It is what it is, whether good or bad. I also enter the highlights of the day before. Short, quick, three-sentence journaling, but it preserves the essence of the day for me.

For many years I drew what was in front of me as I sat at our kitchen table—a vase of roses or hydrangeas, my coffee cup, the playful clock on the wall from a vide grenier. About three years

Daily drawing

ago, inspired by a newfound love of fashion design, I started making a fashion drawing a day. Now, new rules in addition to the old ones: I look for a pattern, shape, silhouette, motif, object, anything, and I task myself to draw a six-piece fashion collection inspired by that choice.

What have I learned? Inspiration can come from any-thing—a kitchen whisk, a garlic bulb, the alphabet! Don't judge, just draw. No editing or judgment at this stage. I coauthored a book called *Creative Sparks*, which details the many ways I look for inspiration. And it truly is all around us.

My drawings can range from great to "meh" to awful. But that's it for the day. It has also been surprising to me that the next day, after absolutely hating what I did the day before, I usually end up seeing merit in the design. I invite you to start a daily art practice!

SWEET RETREAT – MY ART STUDIO

After my morning walk it's off to my studio. My light-filled studio, which overlooks the *Rue des Martineuers* (Street of the Copper Beaters) is my haven. Originally it was to be the guest room, but we noticed a bright village light shone right into the room at night and would make it impossible for guests to sleep. So it became my studio, and now I appreciate the great light I have there day or night. It has two large north-facing windows that have a stunning view of the ancient *Oppidum du Berniquaut* high on the craggy mountain top. This is where a Roman village once stood before the inhabitants came down to resettle close to the River Sor. These two windows also look directly into my

My art studio

neighbor's kitchen, so I made a "curtain" of old slides of my artwork to hang in the window. We like our neighbors, but I think we both appreciate this little bit of privacy, and it's a way for me to make use of all the old slides I have.

This is one of three rooms that have the original tiles of the house from long, long ago, called *tommettes*. They are cracked and uneven but so beautiful. I spent the first summer here renovating them to their original dark red color. It's a process for sure, dictated to me by the chatty woman at the hardware store who insisted I *must* do it right! First clean with soapy water, then rub in the special deep red pigment with a soft cloth. Next, rub on a product called "Brilliance" and finally buff by hand to a

The Coffee Run *wall hanging*

bright sheen. Whoa, it was a lot of work on my hands and knees. But the payoff was worth it.

I have a table set up with my sewing machine to work on my large fabric "fashion lady" wall hangings. And a table set up for my jewelry making.

I've been making mixed-media jewelry since 1991. First with postage stamps from around the world, then adding polymer clay, then adding metal, wire, found objects, and now fabric! I love to find a sideways entry into my jewelry making, a way of being inspired by an outside, sometimes totally unrelated source. My large wall hangings inspire the jewelry I make. Each piece of jewelry has a place to "live" on the wall hanging but can also be taken off and worn.

I'm enjoying making large weirdly proportioned flower brooches right now. Big Bold flowers to wear perhaps sitting on your shoulder. Next up, a long long loooooooong necklace to wear several different ways. Let's hear it for jewelry that is outsized, bold, and verging on unwearable—it makes a statement!

Salut! *wall hanging*

Also in my studio is a beautiful armoire with graceful French curves and inlaid with the famous Revel wood marquetry of flowers and grapevines intertwined in different colors of wood. We found it in a thrift store for thirty euros, and even though I didn't think I needed it, I said, "It's thirty euros—we have to take it!" Now it is stuffed with art supplies and my fabric stash. Escaping to my studio in France is a deep pleasure.

Orange blossom brooch

OUR GARDEN

Next up is to tackle our back garden. After living in New York City and under the redwood trees in California, we never had a chance to garden.

Sunflower brooch

Now, with a sunny backyard in our little village in France, it's time to see if we have green thumbs.

Our backyard is separated from our neighbors by five-foot-tall walls. One wall is beautiful ivy-covered old stones, the other is concrete block that we recently covered with a lovely yellow-gold *chaux* (pigmented plaster). I've started a ceramic flower "art installation" on this wall. I bought old decorative dinner plates and saucers from the flea markets and layered the different sizes to make a multi-layered flower. Attached to the wall, along with copper pipe "stems" and antique silver forks as leaves, these flowers really make this wall special. Along the top of this wall we are growing wisteria that has finally started to bloom.

When we first arrive every year, the garden is a jungle. The weeds have grown chest high and the flowers and fig tree have gone crazy. We can't even see the river behind us.

Flower wall with flea market plates

Dan starts taming things right away so we can start planting the veggies. But our dirt—ugh! The poor-quality dirt is filled with five hundred years of rubble! But that doesn't deter us. Roses and hydrangeas do great even without us knowing anything at all. When we dig down to plant, we find bits of pottery and clay bits, stones, leather shoe soles, bits of wire, old spark plugs—we even dug up a small iron statue of a cherub that had been tarnished to a beautiful patina. It sits on our bedroom fireplace mantle.

But the surprising discovery of one summer came when Dan was transplanting a hydrangea. Digging down, he bumped into something large. He dug and pulled and dug and pulled and eventually dragged up a large piece of metal and glass, which turned out to be a car door with its window, bright yellow with writing on the side advertising a disco that had been in the area in the 1960s! The glass broke upon pulling it out, but the car door is amazing. Who knows what else lurks below! I plan to do an art installation with the car door attached to the wall and clay figures and animals piled into the car.

As soon as we arrive in April or May we rush to our favorite plant man

Our rosy back wall

at the Saturday market in Revel. He always has at least fifteen varieties of tomatoes, and that's where we begin. Having access to fresh tomatoes is a dream to me. But can we grow veggies in our

poor dirt? The first year we bought three bags of good soil, turned them flat, slit open the bag, and planted three tomato plants in each of the bags. Surprise, surprise—we had a bounty of tomatoes! Since then, even in our poor dirt, we have

Our first year tomato crop

33

had success with peppers, eggplants, squash, green beans, and strawberries—but especially tomatoes. Every year we have a huge yield. When we leave each year in late September, I always have about twenty pounds of green tomatoes left. So, what to do? I tried a few recipes using fried green tomatoes, but my most favorite is to make jars and jars of green tomato chutney for the next summer. We enjoy the chutney every day at

Time for green tomato chutney

lunch with cheese and bread, or mixed into hummus. I've got the recipe for you at the end of this chapter!

DAN'S KUMQUAT SAGA

That first summer in our garden, my husband Dan was determined to grow a kumquat tree in our backyard. We found a small one at Auchan—one of our fave French stores. It's similar to a Super Target or Walmart. The tree was full of ripe kumquats—at least seventy-five beautiful small orange fruits. Deliciousness.

We cared for it all summer, picking the fruit off at the end of the summer to make a liqueur that would age all winter. The day before we left France, we shifted the tree (planted in a big pot) to a protected corner of the stone wall, hoping it would survive the winter months. Upon arrival the next year, it had survived, but there were no buds or flowers on the branches. We waited all summer in vain for flowers that would become fruit. Nothing. The next year was the same.

Year four we arrived in April, rushed outside to look at the beloved kumquat tree, and lo and

Dan's kumquat tree

behold it was laden once again with fruit! Many already ripe, some still green and growing. All summer long it produced beautiful orange fruit. Once again, Dan's liqueur business was open. Bottle number two is aging in the kitchen. Here's the recipe.

Kumquat liqueur: Put two liters vodka, one cup sugar, and many sliced kumquats in a large jar or bottle. Shake shake shake and let sit for several months. That's it!

ALWAYS THE FIRST DINNER: DUCK CONFIT!

One of the first meals I make when we arrive in France is duck confit. It is considered one of the finest French dishes and is one of our region's specialties. I was introduced to duck confit several years ago by my village friend Ann Mason, and for me, a person who did not like duck, it was a real culinary revelation. We were invited to Ann's for dinner. When she said she was serving duck, my stomach dropped. I'm just going to have to be polite and eat it, I told myself. My plate arrived with the duck thigh, beautiful roasted potatoes, and French green beans. Oh my, the crispiest skin covered the duck meat, which literally fell off the bone and melted in my mouth. I swooned. "Please, tell me how you make this?" I said to Ann.

She went into her kitchen and brought out a large tin. And surprise, surprise: the Revelois brand of duck confit in a can is the best! All the hard work of *sloooooowly* cooking the duck in its own fat is done for you. Ann then tutored me on how to make this impressive and delicious dish.

First you take the duck legs and thighs out of the can, out of a golden swimming pool of pure duck fat. In a hot skillet, you sauté the duck for a few minutes to release and pour off more of the duck fat. Next, put them skin-side up in a dish and into the oven and bake until the skin is crispy—about 15–20 minutes. *Voilà!*

An added bonus is the pure golden duck fat to be used all summer long. It is a wonderful cooking fat, and believe me, it does not taste ducky at all. I keep it in a container in the freezer and take out what I want when cooking. I sauté veggies, meats—anything that calls for olive oil—in my precious duck fat. And I take home several cans of Revelois duck confit to my home state-side too!

THE CHICKEN WARS

In 2019, upon arrival, we were warned by our lovely neighbor Marie that neighbor Jean-Marc (in between us) now has three chickens. The chickens were running rampant over our two gardens instead of their own! I had already been through the Rooster Wars a few years ago and wasn't relishing this battle.

In 2012 we arrived to find we had a rooster living next door. He would constantly parade back and forth on top of our garden wall, and not only did he crow at 4:00 a.m. but he cockadoodle-dooed all day long. It truly was about to drive me insane. I had three weeks of sleepless nights, and the rooster was so threatening to guests that came for dinner in our garden, they suggested we murder him! We really liked these neighbors, but they only spoke French, and we were not sure how to approach the problem. Should we offer to buy it (and then give it to someone to make *coq au vin?* Ha!) Luckily our dear French friend Antoine talked to them with us. They were already thinking about getting rid of the rooster, as he had started pecking at their three-year-old son. So we reached a quick agreement—they just needed a couple weeks to locate someone to give this beast to. And that did happen.

So now, seven years later, it's the chickens. We looked at our back garden and saw that our lovely mint and many other things in our garden were pecked away. Daily I watched—and photographed—the chickens running around the wall that separates our two properties through a small place near the river that has no barrier. They pecked, pecked, pecked away at our yard, and even tried to get into my kitchen!

Hmm. Not being French—and not knowing the legalities of our situation—we consulted a few friends. Are the chickens allowed to be free-range even if it makes it impossible for us to grow our beloved summer garden? Can we put up a small barrier where there is no wall? We were told we did have a right to put up a barrier.

So Dan built the barrier. It was small—only going from the end of our wall and down to the river, about two feet long and nicely made—tidy, discreet, and at least two feet within our boundary line. We put it up late Thursday afternoon.

That night we peeked from our upstairs window down to the neighbor's backyard. The husband saw our new barrier—not much of a reaction. Good! Then the wife saw the barrier—dramatic angry gestures and shouting, which of course we could not understand. We slipped back away from the window to have dinner, hoping it would calm down. Dan went out to look a bit later and saw that "someone" had not only torn down the barrier but had stomped and crushed it too. GRRR!!!

Off we went the next day to the mayor's office. This is the next step when you have a problem in the village. *Monsieur* le Maire was waiting for us with these words, "I know why you are here—the chickens." We proceeded to have a conversation with him about our rights. Yes, we do have the right to a small barrier, and yes, our neighbor trespassed to tear down our barrier. He told us to put the barrier back up, and he would send a letter saying there were two choices: Our barrier stays up, or our neighbor can make his own chicken enclosure. No free-range!

We walked home and met two friends on the way and explained the situation. Out of the blue one friend said, "Hold the presses—your neighbor gave me his chickens today!!"

"What!" I said.

"Yes! your neighbor gave me his three chickens today."

"Incroyable! Incredible!" I said.

We ran back down to the mayor. "Hold the letter, no need to send!"

When we got home, Dan went to the garden to take down the rest of the crushed barrier. Our neighbor came around the edge of the wall. I was watching nervously from our secret upstairs window and saw them pantomime and speak (bad French on Dan's part), and they both agreed it's okay now and shook hands. We sealed the deal by knocking on their door a few minutes later and presenting them with a bottle of good red wine and my fresh homemade strawberry cake. Chicken wars averted!

RECIPES

CHERRY JAM

Remove pits and stems from 2 lb. of cherries. Put them in a pot with 2 Tbsp. water. Cook over medium heat, stirring occasionally, until the cherries are cooked through—about 10 minutes. Stir in 2 ½ cups sugar and the juice of one lemon. Increase heat to medium-high and cook, stirring often, until cherry mixture has thickened and is very bubbly. With a thermometer, the jam should be between 220 and 225°F. Turn off and stir in 2 drops of almond extract if you want. Ladle into a clean jar. Yum.

Cherry Ginger Scones

Preheat oven to 350°F. Line a baking sheet with parchment paper. Blend together 1 ½ cups whole wheat flour, 2 cups all-purpose flour, and ¾ cup granulated sugar. Add ¾ cup coarsely chopped pitted cherries and 1 cup chopped crystallized ginger. Toss to coat. In another bowl, combine 1 cup heavy cream, ½ cup buttermilk, and 2 Tbsp. lemon zest. Pour into flour mixture and stir until just combined.

Flour your work surface and turn out dough. Knead for 4—6 turns and then press into a large rectangle approximately 1-inch high. Cut in half lengthwise, then cut each half into 4 squares, then each square diagonally into two triangles. Transfer to baking sheet and brush top of each with a little cream and a sprinkling of sugar. Bake 30–35 minutes until golden brown.

Green Tomato Chutney

Place 7 cups green tomatoes roughly chopped, 1 ¼ cups cider vinegar, 1 cup brown sugar, 1 cup raisins, 1 cup chopped onion, 1 tsp. ground ginger, ½ tsp. mustard seeds, 2 tsp. salt, ¼ tsp. ground cloves, a little hot sauce if you like. Bring to a boil. Reduce heat and simmer for 1 ½ hours until thickened, stirring often. Cool slightly and ladle into clean jars, cover, and seal.

Strawberry Bread

Preheat oven to 35°F. Butter and flour a loaf pan. Beat 4 eggs with 1 ½ cups canola oil. Add into this: 3 cups flour sifted with 1 tsp. salt, 1 tsp. baking soda, 1 Tbsp. cinnamon and 2 cups sugar. Stir in 16 ounces fresh or frozen (thawed) sliced strawberries.

Add 1 ½ cups chopped pecans. Pour into your loaf pan. Bake at 350°F for 45 minutes, till golden brown and a toothpick comes out clean.

3.
Village Places and People

Our village café

FOR A VILLAGE OF JUST A COUPLE HUNDRED PEOPLE, we have a unique and varied history starting in the 1300s, through WWII and the village's resistance fighters, and now evolving into an artisan village. Join me as I show you around my village and introduce you to a cast of interesting characters, my friends.

LE CYRANO CAFÉ

My favorite café is Le Cyrano in our medieval village of Durfort. Le Cyrano is the heart of our village—both literally and symbolically. It sits in the town square and is the central gathering place for the village.

From Le Cyrano, you can literally watch village life go by. There is indoor and outdoor seating to watch the Thursday night *boules* games, wave to neighbors, welcome visitors, play cards while sipping wine or a *café crème*, have a quick snack—a *croque monsieur,* crepe, chorizo sandwich, quiche—gather to hear a local music event, read the latest notice of who or what will be coming to town, quietly sketch or journal, and of course, get the latest gossip.

In French cafés you can sit as long as you want with your drink of choice. Many times the owner will drop off a plate of olives, chips, or slices of sausage. At breakfast time you can even bring in your own croissant or pain au chocolat to have along with your coffee. There's no pressure to leave, and when you are ready to go you walk inside and pay.

Le Cyrano had been run for many, many years by one couple. A few years ago they decided to close. Our village was without a café for over a year. It was as if the pulse of the village had stopped. Luckily, Elodie, the new owner, reopened, and once again we had our heart of the village back.

As an American living in the village during the summer, this has been the place for me to go to meet other villagers and let them know how much I enjoy being a real part of the village. It's a relaxed place to just "be" and to be open to spur-of-the-moment decisions. One time we were there with new friends, it was getting close to dinner time (which I had not started yet), and it just felt right to say, "Come on up to our house and we'll all make dinner together." It was a wonderful evening and a way to get to know new friends. I invite you to come to our charming village and I'll take you down to our beloved café!

ANN AND PORTO BLANC

Ann Mason has been spending her summers in our village for some twenty-odd years. She is a British silk painter extraordinaire, and she and her husband Peter were the heart and soul of this village for many years. Ann and Peter had weekly dinner parties and always made sure that French and English speakers were both invited.

We first met them through Gwen Gibson, the creator and owner of La Cascade. Many a night was spent over good food and conversation on the outdoor terrace at La Cascade. The fragrant rose canopy up above us, the River Sor flowing beside, and the Armagnac (brandy) flowed too!

Ann offers a two-hour silk painting class to the visiting work-shops at La Cascade. And she, being fluent in French, also gives a free weekly "English for French speakers" class at our Le Cyrano café. Peter was a wonderful pen-and-ink/watercolor artist who offered a weekly drop-in drawing workshop for adults and kids at their studio on our street. He was determined to paint every house in our sweet village. He completed twenty-eight before he died a few years ago. The whole village treasures his memory, and he is the only Englishman buried in the village cemetery. His paintings live on through postcards available at our café, along with his watercolor book of the houses of Durfort.

One of Ann and Peter's favorite places to "winter" was Portugal. In a beautiful B&B not too far from Porto, she discovered *porto blanc* (white port). It is made in the Duoro Valley—a gorgeous area steeply terraced and patterned with miles and miles of vineyards. Upon Ann's return to our village café, she asked

Elodie for a porto blanc. Elodie shook her head. "*Non, nous n'avons pas*" (No, we don't have any). Ann is a huge supporter of our village café: She goes down midmorning for a coffee and almost every afternoon to meet friends (like me) for an afternoon drink.

Elodie promised to get a bottle to have on hand for her. Soon after, Ann introduced me to porto blanc. It's popular as an aperitif, on the sweeter side, and is meant to be ice cold and slowly sipped. It's delicious even if you think you don't like sweet wines. Soon friends and workshop participants would notice the lovely light golden liquid that Ann and I were sipping. And as we introduced porto blanc to more and more people that came to our village, the café started having to buy cases! It is now a favorite village drink. Much enjoyed in the late afternoon after a creative studio session or a day of working hard.

MY CAFÉ SINGER DREAMS

In 2017 Ann Mason's stepson Rich visited our village. He's a very shy man who had been studying the saxophone for quite a while and was very good. Rich wanted to get used to playing for an audience, so I suggested he play for us in our then-empty living room (we had not furnished it yet except for a couple chairs). The music and acoustics were wonderful. He played mostly

My café singer dream comes true

American classics, Frank Sinatra, Tony Bennett, Latin faves, etc. Ann and I looked at each other as we were swaying to the tunes, and being possessed for a brief moment I said, "Next summer, we must perform at Le Cyrano café! We'll sing, and Rich will play!"

Early the following summer—with this fleeting suggestion long out of my head—Ann received from Rich a sax backing tape of many songs so we could start rehearsing. WHAT! We had forgotten all about it, but not Rich. He had his reservation to come to France and was ready for us. We felt we had to go through with the concert now and rushed down to the café to speak with Elodie, the owner. With a very surprised look, she said okay, and we picked a date.

Next on the agenda, Ann and I needed to recruit a couple more ladies, as we were not singers and needed safety in numbers. First our dear friend Severine, a French friend who speaks a little English. Then Ann's daughter-in-law Kate. Time was tight so we had two short rehearsals of our eight songs. Well...we had fun during rehearsals, but we definitely were not that good—a bit embarrassing! But that's okay, as it was really for Rich to have the opportunity to play. And we weren't letting anyone know we were doing this.

The night of the "concert" we were a bit late, as we thought, *oh gosh, maybe we should vocally warm up.* We finally got to the village café about fifteen minutes late. AND it was packed with friends and locals all coming to see the new lounge singers. Up at the front beside the old bar, the music stands and speakers were set up. Rich seemed very nervous and set his music stand so that his back was to the audience. "Nuh-uh," I said. "You've got to at least turn sideways! This is your night!"

Our audience sat in the new orange café chairs and comfy sofas and even spilled out to the outdoor seating under bright blue umbrellas. Here were our neighbors from our street, friends from neighboring villages, older residents curious about what was going on, and little kids running back and forth giving us a thumbs-up. And off we went. Our eight songs—including "Girl from Ipanema," "Fever," "Hit the Road Jack," "*Quizas*" (Perhaps), and "Cry me a River," were a huge hit. We each had our "lounge singer" personalities. Severine was very nervous about singing in English and had her nose buried in our songbook. Kate, who is quite shy, was a good singer but quite reserved. Ann was nonchalantly leaning her elbow on the bar, quite at ease. And then me. I was unaware, but I was quite the "swayer" and quite animated. At least that's what several of the villagers said. "Dayle! Oooooh!" and then they would sway side to side with big grins.

"What are you talking about?" I asked. And then I saw the video. I definitely was having a good time and embracing my dream to sing in a club. An encore was requested—which, of course, we hadn't prepared—so we sang "Fever" again. Most of the French knew it and enthusiastically sang along with us, hitting the table, *thump thump,* every time we sang "Fever!" (*thump thump*). Great night—dream come true!

LA TABLE DE DURFORT

Our village has been waiting for years for a restaurant to open. In the summer of 2018, this dream finally became a reality. La Table de Durfort opened its doors as a moderately priced gourmet restaurant here in our small village. The renovated corner spot right off the village square is beautiful, a simple elegant atmosphere decorated in muted tans and grays. Outside is a lovely outdoor patio covered with ivy and climbing roses—light pink, red-and-white "candycane roses," and deep magenta. Along the side of the patio is the chef's herb garden. Each table has a vase of sweet tiny roses along with the glistening glassware and plates. La Table is owned by partners Chef Julien and Louisa. The restaurant offers two menus plus à la carte, and the menu changes every few weeks. You can choose either a two-course or three-course meal for lunch or dinner.

Dan and I and our neighbor went a month after they opened. Oh wow—beautiful presentation! Art on a plate, with fantastic creativity and flavors. I started with an *entrée* (appetizer) of delicious duck confit in flaky pastry bundles topped with a lovely sauce of mache. Mache is a soft green, also known as lamb's lettuce, and grows in small rosette-shaped bunches. It has a distinct, sweet taste. The duck confit melted in my mouth as I bit into the crunchy savory pastry.

My *plat* (main dish) was a *ballotine* of chicken in a Comté cheese sauce with beautiful veggies. In a ballotine, the chicken is deboned and rolled into a bundle, soft and tender to slice. The aroma of the Comté cheese sauce wafted up, nutty and fruity. Baby carrots and small golden potatoes roasted and glazed with butter completed the plate. The highlight of the meal for me was my dessert (it usually is). As our server brought dessert, I could already smell the rich chocolate that would soon ooze out of the middle of my *fondant au chocolat* (molten chocolate cake). New to me (as I *always* order this dessert and it usually comes with whipped cream) was the salted caramel sauce—the combination of sweet and salty complimented the rich chocolate perfectly.

There were few customers that weeknight so we ooohed and ahhhed and yummmmed frequently out loud. As we finished the last bites, the chef thanked us with a complimentary glass of champagne. Cheers—*Salut*—to La Table de Durfort! The evening was magical, and we are so lucky to have this restaurant in our village now.

CHEF GIGI

Gigi has been the chef/owner of Le Tournesol (The Sunflower) restaurant in the nearby village of Soreze for forty years. I was stunned when I found this out. Her staff is small: Gigi, two servers, and I hope someone to help with dishes! The restaurant serves lovely traditional French food and regional specialties at moderate prices. Among them: cassoulet, duck confit, *souris d'agneau* (lamb shank), omelets, and my favorite dessert—fondant au chocolat. The restaurant's old stone walls are covered by inspiring and unusual art of local artists that Gigi handpicks. There are five rooms of unique paintings, sculptures, and mixed-media wall art. I was honored to have a four-month exhibit in 2018 of my textile wall hangings of whimsical fashion ladies and jewelry.

Gigi greets each person as they enter the restaurant in her crisp white chef's coat. She's tiny but has a strong presence. I have been taking my La Cascade workshop groups here for a "French restaurant experience" since 2004. As we enter, Gigi shakes hands with all my students and gives me a once over (I try to dress up for her). *"Bonjour, ma belle,"* she always says.

One night that our group went happened to fall on her birthday. I wrapped up one of my brooches that I hoped she would like, and my workshop gals, along with our friends Ann and Peter, practiced a famous French song called "*Le Tournesol.*" Our plan was to sing it to her in the restaurant. We arrived all dressed up and looking gorgeous, and Gigi greeted us at the door. She loved the brooch and offered us all an aperitif. Most of us chose my favorite new drink, porto blanc. For our main dishes, we all ordered something different; it's a wonderful introduction to classic French food.

Gigi came to the table after our dessert and we sang "*Bonne Anniversaire,*" (Happy Birthday). It's the same tune as the American version. Then we dove into our jaunty "Le Tournesol." She looked surprised—well, a bit shocked—but sat down with us and truly seemed to enjoy this small American celebration of her special day. As she left our table she told us to wait, as she had something special. After a few minutes, a tray was brought out with a small *boule* (ball) of basil sorbet for each of us—it was divine.

Soon after this special night, Gigi told me that she never gets invited for a homemade dinner because everyone is afraid to cook for her! That sent my friend Ann Mason and me into action. We decided that every summer we would alternate having Gigi over for dinner. Ann volunteered to go first, and we set the date. She thought it would be interesting to cook her blackened chicken wings with lemon and garlic that one MUST eat with fingers. We both wondered if beautiful Gigi would be up for that. The night of the dinner Ann brought out the big pan of chicken, roasted garlic, and sliced lemons straight from the oven to the middle of the table. Not only did we all, including Gigi, dive right in, she did so with great gusto and enthusiasm! We had a wonderfully messy meal together.

The next year was my turn. As the date approached I was getting really nervous. I couldn't decide what to cook. I finally decided to go Asian in the hope that it was something that Gigi didn't ordinarily cook. I started off with an apéro featuring pickled radishes and onions. For the entrée, a crisp green salad and my roasted shallot dressing. For the main course, I decided on peach and ginger glazed chicken with coconut rice and roasted cauliflower. The day of my dinner I prepped and cooked all day and set up a lovely table in our garden. I trepidatiously presented my food. Gigi could not be a more wonderful guest. She gasped in delight. She ate everything with great enjoyment, asked for seconds, asked for recipes, asked for a jar of the pickled radishes, and made sure that I felt confident as a cook. What a wonderful experience to get to know a real French chef and what their life is like.

ROGER: SEES ALL, KNOWS ALL

You can see Roger walking around our village with his tiny dog, Flora, almost any time of the day. He is a short man with bowed legs and large black-framed glasses that magnify his eyes to twice their size, and he always has a big friendly smile. We meet early every morning as I start my exercise walk up the mountain. He speaks in rapid-fire French, which I cannot understand, but now we have a routine. I ask him to speak slowly please, which he does, while emphasizing each word with a rhythmic pat on my shoulder.

If you need to know *anything* about the village, Roger is your man. What's happening at the café or community room, what the weather is for the week, how long the winds will blow, why my grapevine is not making grapes, why there is water coming up through my floor, what houses are for sale—he knows all. He is such a trusted member of the village that most of the owners have given him a spare key to their houses. He'll water your flowers, let the electric and water meter men in to read your meter, check to make sure your shutters are closed during a storm. Whatever and whenever you need help, he is there.

Roger started working at the bakery that was once here in our village decades ago when he was six years old! I don't know the story of how that came to be, but he worked there for fourteen years. Then he took care of an older man in the village, and when this grateful man died, he left his house to Roger. Roger has a huge vegetable and flower garden, provides fresh flowers in the church, and often delivers beans, potatoes, and tomatoes to us lucky villagers. Now in his seventies, he has worked alongside William, the village handyman, for over twenty years. He is a very special and much-appreciated man in our village.

A SPECIAL GEM, THE DURFORT CHURCH

We have a precious little jewel of a church in our small village of two hundred—the Saint-Etienne Church. Built in the thirteenth century, it was completely (except for the choir) destroyed during the Wars of Religion in the 1500s. The nave was rebuilt in the seventeenth century, and the building was raised and vaulted in the late 1800s. As I write, it is being renovated by a group of our villagers. The walls that had been plastered over are being returned to the beautiful white stone originally used in the construction. The antique Joan of Arc statue now has a special place at the front of the church, and the ceiling has been refurbished to the original gorgeous blue and white. The old stained-glass windows have been replaced with ones by a contemporary glass artist; spirals of colorful glass mosaics reflect squares of color throughout the church. They blend nicely with the historic parts of the church. I like the combination of old and new.

The church bells ring hourly day and night. The bells at noon ring fifty times—this shows how important the noon-time meal has been throughout history. For the field and copper workers, this was the main meal of the day and not to be missed. Roger provides fresh flowers every week in handcrafted vases that are placed around the church. One of the first things he does every morning is unlock the church so that it is open to villagers and tourists. Our church is not used for mass anymore but for small music concerts. I always bring friends and my workshop participants here to witness firsthand the exquisite acoustics. One of my students gave us an impromptu concert of Sarah McLachlan's "Angel" as we sat in the church. She truly had the voice of an angel.

OUR COPPER HISTORY AND VILLAGE OF ARTISANS

Durfort, which translates as "hard and strong," has been making copperware since the fourteenth century. The village at one time had fourteen mills along our river, and as the textile mills closed, the village converted those mills to copper-making studios. The artisans pounded out copper ingots from recycled scrap copper into beautiful shapes, and Durfort became nationally well-known for its copperware. The three residential streets that radiate from Le Cyrano café and the town square have unique char-

Village copper store

acteristics. Each of the streets has a small stream running down the middle that was once used in the copper-making process to quench the copper pots after being shaped. The beautiful homes on these streets, both large and small, were once the copper ateliers for refining the shape of the copper pots and adding decoration. There is still a working studio in the village, along with an interesting copper museum chronicling the history of copper making in the village, a history that continues on.

In our little village, there was a mayor who reigned for forty-seven years. And not a nice man. There were rumors that he was involved in a murder in the village square! Finally in 2015, his reign was broken and a new mayor emerged. Our new mayor's great-uncle had been mayor during the World War II and had been betrayed and taken away by the Nazis. In fact, most of the men in our village were taken away and killed. Many of the houses on the riverside, including our house, harbored resistance fighters in their attics. There were small makeshift bridges built across the River Sor, and the fighters could run across quickly and hide in the Montagne Noire. But one day in 1944, this did not happen. The men of the village were taken away forever. The mayor's wife at that time stepped in and became the first and only female mayor.

Our village has a small central square surrounded by *la Marie* (the mayor's building) and several artisan shops. We've been a destination village to buy copper for decades, and now we can also boast of several artisan studios. First are the two remaining *cuivre* (copper) shops. Even today, people come here from all over to buy Durfort copper in the Pierre Vergnes and Les Cuivres d'Elodie copper ateliers, as well as less expensive copper pieces made in North Africa but using the classic old French designs. Pierre Vergnes has on staff our good friend Antoine, who can re-tin and refurbish old copper pots to make them usable again. He also creates beautiful and unique custom-made copper, brass, and silver jewelry and sculptural art.

Next door to the café is our local glass studio: wine glasses, sherbet dishes, plates, jewelry—all handmade in their kiln. Crys Parker Creations, fine handmade leather goods, is right next to the copper shop. Didier, the owner, makes exquisite leather purses, belts, jackets, and other items. It's definitely a place of inspiration.

My friend Marie-Jo owns a sweet boutique, ReCreation, right next to la Marie, that features her fine woodwork and other local artists' jewelry, ceramics, and children's toys. The Vannerie features handmade baskets made by Brigitte, who also offers workshops. And a new gallery, Hello!, has opened around the corner, featuring paintings and sculptures from regional artists. Lots to explore in tiny Durfort!

LEO OF SOREZE

Leo was a very special man who lived in the village next to ours for several summers. He was the Assistant Dean of Animation at CalArts in Los Angeles and a wonderful artist in his own right. A small but feisty man, he was a gourmet

The famous Leo blue dress

chef, diva, fantastic conceptual artist, curmudgeon, and generous, heart-filled man. He was stubborn, a ball of energy—and contradictions, as you can see! We spent many a time with him hiking, having delicious meals, seeing his grad students' films, and having lots of great conversations about art and life.

My favorite Leo memory has to do with a pale blue organza dress from the 1950s. We were at a vide grenier (flea market) buzzing with energy, usually a place to meet our like-minded friends. Dan and I had literally just plunked down our life savings on a French house a few days before and were leaving France in a couple days. The vendors lined the streets of the quaint village and it was fun to just meander from booth to booth, dreaming of what I might get for our French house if the sale actually went through. And we were happy to bump into our good friend Leo. He invited us to a film that night, which we politely declined, and I have to say he was quite angry that we would not change the plans we already had for that evening. He walked off in a diva-esque huff, shaking his head and the index finger of his right hand as if I had been a bad student. Dan and I looked at each other with a shrug. Oh well. That's Leo.

A bit later Leo found me at the flea market and said, "I have found a dress that you must buy."

I was a bit peeved at his behavior before and said, "No, Leo, I don't wear dresses very much and we have just hopefully bought a house—I am not buying a dress."

Leo said, "I am telling you, you must buy this dress."

I again said, "No, I am not buying a dress."

Again he said, "I am telling you, you *must* buy this dress."

I caved and said, "Leo, if the dress is five euros, I will buy it."

Leo took me by the arm and hurriedly escorted me to the booth of the Dress. With a sweeping arm gesture, Leo said, *"Madam, la robe, s'il vous plait!"*

Madam dramatically brought forth a baby blue filmy dress, organza with raised flocked black designs and a Peter Pan collar. I was a bit shocked, as I didn't think it would fit me, and where would I wear such a dress made for a princess from the 1950s?

But I said, "Madam, how much is the dress?"

"Ten euros," she said.

"Will you take five euros?" I said.

"Non!" Madam said. And I hurriedly left the booth before being thrown out.

"Leo, I am sorry but I cannot buy the dress."

End of conversation.

He was furious with me and turned away. Dan and I also turned and left.

About five minutes later, Leo found me and quietly handed me the dress, which now hangs proudly on my studio wall. In memory of my dear friend Leo.

METAMORPHOSIS: A VILLAGE OF MURALS

We have a new mayor, and what a change he has brought to the village. Lots of enthusiasm and energy and a willingness to try almost anything that benefits our village and makes it better. We try new festivals (last year was a country western dance weekend), have potluck dinners in the street, and new artwork has sprouted up all over. Our sweet village, which for decades, even centuries, has been known for copper making, is starting

Durfort Montagne Noire mural

to change. Even though there are still two stores with the famous Durfort copper, we have now been recognized as an official Artisans Village. There are new copper and steel sculptures in the village square that honor the past but in a contemporary style. The River Sor is home to three bronze hippopotamuses gleefully floating near the old Roman stone bridge. And the mayor's new project: wonderful arty murals that are being painted around the village.

The first commission was a large mural on the side of a two-story building in the town square. Two artists—one French, Tian, and one English, Johnny— created the huge mural. The scaffolding was up all summer and we watched the whimsical deer, mushrooms, ladybugs, spiders, wild boars, dancing snakes, and other flora and fauna of our Montagne Noire come to life. I have to say it was very controversial. The village was divided on it— some loved it, some hated it. Even though it was not my usual style, I did love it, if only for the fact that if I drove into a village and saw this huge mural, it would compel me to stop and look around. What kind of arty village would have this?

Copper Man *mural*

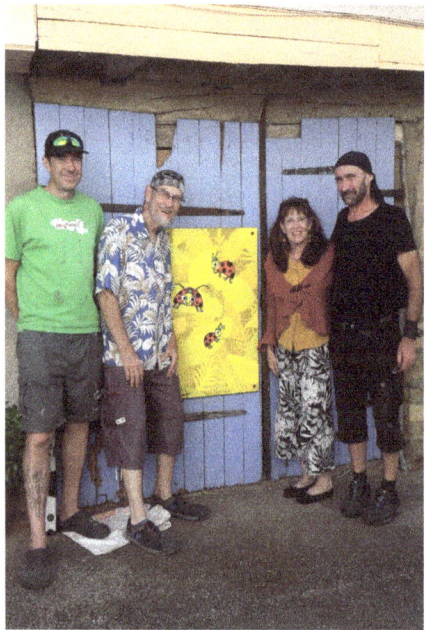

Our ladybug mural with Dan, Dayle, and the artists

60

Soon we heard that Tian and Johnny were willing to paint murals on the garage doors and doorways in the village. Dan and I were thrilled and asked for a ladybug to be painted on our garage. Now our brightly colored red-and-black *coccinelle* stands proudly with perhaps thirty other murals in the streets. We have become the Village of Murals!

MAGIC WATER

At the foot of our village street, you cross the old Roman bridge and enter a shady glen along the River Sor. There are picnic benches for all to use and a faded but colorful statue of Mary from the 1800s, who watches over the area. But the main attraction is our village fountain. The large carved-limestone slab is embedded in the ancient stone wall along the embankment. The water flows endlessly from the bronze fountain tap in the shape of a fish. The water originates from a spring high up on the Montagne Noire and is tested regularly for safety. There is a dedication carved at the top honoring Madame Malignon, who was the first and only female mayor of Durfort. We heard that the fountain was the dedicated meeting place for young lovers during World War II.

We were at first surprised to find out that this is where most villagers get their water. Then we tasted it: always ice cold, delicious, and said to have magical properties. Dan goes down once a week to fill a large container so that we always have the magic water for guests and ourselves.

On weekends the fountain is the busiest place in the village. People come from all over the region for the Durfort water. There are cars and station wagons lined up with large crates of bottles ready and waiting to be filled with Durfort water. We feel very lucky that we are just two minutes away from this special place.

OUR SPECIAL PAINTING

Our good friends Allan and Lesley have introduced us to so many wonderful people in France. We've met a whole community of artists through them, and they are our best biking and camping buddies. Allan is a fantastic watercolor artist. He offers workshops and online videos that teach his techniques. When we go camping, we most often find Allan sitting alone, quietly sketching a beautiful scene at whatever village we are visiting. Lesley creates digital art and is a fantastic chef. We have had many of our best meals ever at her lunch and dinner gatherings. Their huge patio looks out over the countryside and is lined with three different varieties of fig trees. (Another place for me to come pick!)

I try out my cooking skills at least once a summer on Chef Lesley. I don't really compare to her but try my best. One summer's lunch I started with a small apéro before we sat down to eat. I made something kind of strange—pickled grapes. In my defense, I had found this recipe and it sounded new and interesting. Interesting but weird! Luckily I also made my yummy tomato cheddar tart and finished off with melon sorbet. While we were chatting, unbeknownst to us, Allan had snapped a photo of a part of the garden and the back of our house with the blue shutters and climbing rose bushes of red, coral, and "peppermint" red-and-white stripes. As a surprise, he painted an original watercolor painting from the photo. I had it made into a larger version on canvas. You will love looking at Allan's art, classes, and tutorials at www.allankirk.art.

RECIPES

Melted Cheese, Onion, and Sausage Open-face Café Sandwich

Mince 2 small onions and sauté in a little olive oil for 20 minutes till browned and caramelized. Add a little salt and pepper and 1 tsp. of brown sugar and 1 Tbsp. of balsamic vinegar. Sauté another 5 minutes or so till sugar and vinegar are incorporated. Meanwhile, ready your sausages. I use chipolatas in France, which are a thin pork sausage with herbs and spices. You can use the sausage of your choice. Either grill, bake, or sauté them till done. Cut a nice ciabatta-style bread into sandwich slices. Spread the onions on the bottom of the bread. Slice the sausage down the middle, butterfly open, and put on top of the onions. Top the sausage with a big handful of gruyère cheese and some fresh thyme. Broil the open-face sandwich for 2–4 minutes, but watch carefully so it doesn't burn!

Gooey Chocolate Cake

Preheat oven to 350°F. Butter a 9 ½ inch springform pan and dust with flour. Melt 1 ¾ sticks butter in a pan over low heat and add 7 ounces semisweet chocolate. Stir until everything is melted together. Remove from heat and add 4 eggs, 1 ¼ cups sugar, ⅓ cup whole wheat flour, and a pinch of salt while you keep stirring. Scrape batter into prepared pan and bake 15–20 minutes. Cake will be moist and gooey in the center.

Pickled Radishes

Cut radishes into two and a small white onion into slices. Pack a clean canning jar with the radishes and the onions to the top. In a saucepan bring ¾ cup red wine vinegar, ¼ cup sugar, 1 tsp. salt, 7 whole black peppercorns, 1 tsp. cumin, 1 tsp. coriander, and 1 cinnamon stick to a boil. Boil and stir for 1 minute until sugar dissolves. Pour vinegar over the radishes and, if not full to the top, add water. Close the lid, turn upside down, and let cool. Radishes will be done in 24 hours. Keep in refrigerator.

Tomato Cheddar Tart

Buy or make a tart or pie crust. I like to use puff pastry. Preheat oven to 400°F. Line your tart or pie pan with parchment paper.

Slice 3-5 tomatoes (or lots of cherry tomatoes) into rounds approximately ¼ inch thick. Lay onto paper towels to drain for an hour. Blot dry.

Mix ¾ cup grated cheddar (or cheese of your choice), ¼ cup grated parmesan, ⅓ cup mayonnaise, and a bit of salt and pepper in a bowl. Spread over the bottom of the tart pastry. (I like to add a layer of sliced chorizo, ham, or pepperoni on top of the cheese/mayo mixture.) Top with all the tomato slices. Season with black pepper. Sprinkle with some chopped basil and finish off with a bit more cheese. Bake 40–45 minutes until golden brown.

4.
Whirlwind Village Life

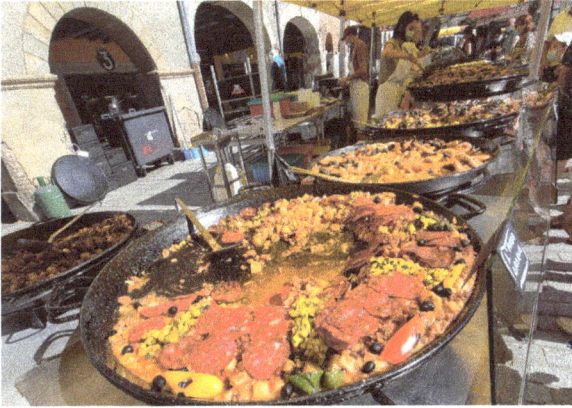

Feast at the Revel market

LIFE IN OUR SMALL VILLAGE IS QUITE DIFFERENT from our life in big cities in the US, but not in the way you might expect. From the moment we arrive home in Durfort our social calendar gets filled up to the brim with places to go and village activities with friends and neighbors. From markets to special dinners, festival committee meetings to the festivals themselves, it's a cornucopia of special and memorable experiences.

THE FANTASTIC REVEL MARKET

Saturday market. The skies are bright blue and a warm breeze softly blows through the village. After a hard winter of endless wind and rain, everyone is out shopping for the glorious veggies, fruits, and other local delights. Revel's timbered covered square was built in the 1300s, and there has been a Saturday market here ever since. This market, five minutes from us, has been named one of the 100 Most Beautiful Markets in France and certainly lives up to the honor. What better place to buy what I need for my next dinner party!

Under and around the central square are vendors from the region

Heirloom tomatoes at market

selling gorgeous mounds of fresh produce, olives, breads, spices, cheese, pastries, sausage, tapenades, rotisserie chickens, roasted potatoes, huge plates of bouillabaisse and paella, flowers and plants, fresh herbs and spices, and more—a feast for the eyes as well as the taste buds. Everything is artfully arranged and the pull to sketch and take photos cannot be ignored. There is so much inspiration in the colors I see in the ripe apricots, tomatoes still on the vine, fresh ground spices, and the beautiful white-to-green asparagus. I want to get back in my art studio and mix a color palette inspired by these colors!

The market continues down the streets that spoke off the central square and end two blocks later at the ring road that circles

Revel. Here are the vendors with everything else you could want: clothes, baskets, fabric, linens, jewelry, purses, shoes—even a hardware store vendor and a man selling new sewing machines.

The crowd is filled with energy, greeting friends old and new and gathering at the seven cafés and brasseries that surround the central square for a café au lait and a pastry.

Each Saturday, I look for what special seasonal fruits and veggies have arrived. Strawberries first. Cherries are just starting in now too. Then *groseilles* (red and black currants). My favorite strawberries so far this year are the wild *fraises des bois* (of the woods). These berries are small, pale red, sweet, and aromatic— absolutely delish.

We are growing strawberries, too, in our garden. Last year they took over one whole raised bed, so this year we are replanting them in a hanging system made with a plastic rain gutter hanging on the wall below our wisteria vine.

I just made a delicious ice cream with fresh strawberries, for which you'd need a small ice cream maker. I love our Donvier. I used a combination of cream and coconut milk, then added the fresh berries and their juices. Before I added the berries I "softened" them. You can sprinkle a little sugar on to release the juices or put in the oven for a few minutes—"roast" them a little, so to speak. I added a bit of sugar (or honey) and a little vanilla until I liked the balance of sweet and fruity. Then into the machine, and voilà!

FRENCH DINNER PARTIES

One of the joys of living in a small village is participating in meals with friends and neighbors. French dinner parties are a thing unto themselves. Sitting around a big table, sharing food, conversation, storytelling, and debates, it is a time to be savored. Most dinners start about 7:00 p.m. and can go well past midnight. Food is eaten slowly with time in between courses to digest (and talk more!)

After a couple years of being invited to dinners with French friends, I decided it was time for me to throw one myself. It's a bit complicated; there are rules spoken and unspoken, and I was nervous. But I approached it with the idea that I would do the best I could with good humor and hoped they would understand any faux pas!

I covered our wooden outdoor table with my golden yellow Provençal tablecloth of olives and vines intertwined with bright red poppies. Our hydrangeas—white, violet blue, and pink— were in high bloom, and the basil and other herbs were spilling over onto the patio. I cut a few of our candy cane striped roses for the center of the table. We were surrounded by the soft sounds of the river flowing right at the end of the garden. Dusk came at almost 10:00 p.m., and I had lots of candles ready for that part of the evening.

Right before my guests arrived, I set out the apéro—this means drinks and nibbles. I had special peanuts enrobed in a barbecue coating, a plate of Spanish chorizo chiffonade (paper-thin slices), and, of course, olives from the Revel market. Porto blanc was at the ready, as was a nice chilled rosé. More elaborate apéros would feature kirs (white wine and cassis syrup) and champagne. And more extensive nibbles—perhaps duck pâtés, cornichons, goat cheese stuffed peppers, mussels. There is an aisle in the grocery store devoted just to apéro snacks. It's always located right across from the wine aisle—of course!

Our friends arrive and wander our small garden to see what we are growing, and then we sit and sip by the river; it's a time to just chit chat and catch up a bit. I can relax a little bit during the apéro, but then it's into high gear and into the kitchen.

It's time for the first course (called an entrée in France). I have the small plates laid out and ready to receive, hopefully in an "arty" way—the slice of tomato cheddar tart I made alongside a slice of roasted red pepper. I yell out the kitchen door, "*À table!*" (Time to come to the table.) And we do. The dinner party really begins.

I've got a bit of a problem. I don't have enough plates to serve all the courses. The entrée, cheese, and dessert courses all use the same size plates, so I must wash dishes in between all the courses. I don't want the guests to sit around too long, though there is always friendly chatter (or a good healthy debate) going on. But I came up with a unique solution. I asked our good friends Jacob and Edith—both musicians—to provide in-between-course entertainment! They arrived with guitars, a keyboard, a sound system, and even songs printed out so all could join in. When I give the signal, they wander over to their instruments and I rush into the kitchen.

Now the large dinner plates are laid out for me to add my tried and tested baked salmon, roasted cauliflower, and balsamic-glazed carrots. The salmon recipe is easy and superb (find it at the end of this chapter). I've got a little bit of time now to sit and enjoy the party before the next frantic run to the kitchen. It's so lovely to be outdoors; the sun is starting to set, giving the sky a marbled pink-and-orange glow, in contrast to the bright green of the mountain trees on the other side of the river. Friends are leaning back in their chairs, feeling relaxed and maybe undoing a belt notch or top button. There are still two courses to go!

I give the music signal and up jump Edith and Jacob. This course is easier, as I made it in advance. It's a simple green salad to cleanse the palate and a cheese plate with a freshly sliced baguette. There are rules about the cheese course. No more than three selections (What? That's too bad—I love many!) and you never take seconds. However, I notice my guests are passing the plate around a second time. Ha!

One more musical interlude as I wash the cheese plates so they can become the dessert plates. Dessert can be wonderful chocolate dishes, fruit tarts, small cakes, sorbet or ice creams with a simple cookie, crème brulee, granitas, or *profiteroles*. On and on and on. I serve a ball of cassis sorbet with a coconut cookie. Oh, but wait, it's not really the last course. Still to come—coffee (or tea), chocolates, and homemade liqueurs. More conversation and more music until we hear the church bell ring at 1:00 a.m.

VILLAGE NIGHTS WITH ANN AND PETER

Many years ago our dear friends Ann and Peter started an annual summer event in our village called Poetry and Pizza. About twenty of us gathered in their upstairs dining room for an evening of shared poetry and, of course, food and wine. Their dining room is really only made for eight, but we always found a way to make a circle of chairs for all.

This event attracted all ages. Adults came with favorite poems they loved over the years. Teens from the village came armed with their own written or favorite poetry. Some villagers came with poems in French that they were willing to translate for the English speakers. Many came who didn't even read or like poetry. Piles of poetry books in the center of the dining room table were made available for all.

We started by picking numbers out of Peter's straw hat—this determined the order of reading. Then we all gathered in the circle of chairs with wine, water, or soda in hand. The hour passed by quickly—some poems were hopeful, beautiful, or hilarious, and many were relevant to today even if written fifty years ago. It was a shared celebration of the beauty of language. Then pizza time! Several pizzas were readied in the oven along with a salad or perhaps a small dessert. Then another round of poetry. Pizza and Poetry—a special time shared together in our special village.

Ann and Peter often threw an apéro for the whole village. In front of their house is Place de Sol (sun), a wide-open spot surrounded by chestnut trees and with a somewhat out-of-place small rectangular pond. This shallow pond was once part of the copper-making process and also served as the earliest communal laundry before the washing machine came along. Now it serves as the perfect way to chill wine, beer, and other drinks. They hang by strings for easy pulling out when needed.

There were two tables of gorgeous food contributed by the villagers—a real international feast: the usual nuts and French cheeses, marinated mussels, a Spanish potato and onion tortilla. Penny brought a vegetarian quiche, Rachid brought his wife's special Moroccan-style pizza, and I brought American deviled eggs.

Peter had hired a local accordionist to play for the party. He was an older jolly man, white-haired and with suspenders straining over his belly. He stood under the shade of the tree joyfully swaying, fingers running up and down the keys as he played old French waltzes, polkas, and other jaunty tunes. Peter, always ready for a good time, grabbed me, and he and I danced a wild waltz around the place. French, British, American, Irish, Moroccan—all gathered to chat together in whatever common language they could (including pantomime—the universal language). A few of the older couples got up to dance the musette, rapidly twirling as they did in older times.

Now for the main event! Peter, with a sly smile on his face, brought out plastic kazoos that he had hidden away. Six of us jumped up, laughing, as we accompanied the accordionist as he played "When the Saints Come Marching In" and "Roll out the Barrel." The villagers joined in singing these universally known songs in French and English. And the Durfort Kazoo Orchestra was born that night!

The infamous kazoo orchestra

RESTAURANT ROW ON RUE DES MARTINEURS

Some of you may remember the progressive-style dinners of the past. I can remember my parents having them in the cul-de-sac of our suburban neighborhood. Each house was responsible for one of the courses, ending with drinks and dancing at our house. I can see myself in the hallway spying on my parents and their friends as they danced in our living room where the furniture had been moved out earlier in the day. This last week, here in Durfort, we had a number of wonderful cooks on our street—either permanent residents or summer visitors. I decided it would be fun to do a progressive dinner with entertainment at each stop. I called it Restaurant Row on Rue des Martineurs. I suggested that each host tell a story, recite a poem, or sing a song during their course. This was met with total silence and no takers. Okay! So, Peter came up with the idea that we would have the kazoo orchestra play an appropriate song at each course. Peter gathered the kazoos for himself, Ann, and me. Wanting to sound as professional as possible, we even scheduled two rehearsals.

First stop, the apéro, where all ten of us gathered at the lovely shaded area by the village fountain. We were surrounded by the sounds of the cool, pure, ever-flowing fountain water and the waterfalls of the River Sor. Nese has been the chef at La Cascade for seventeen years. Of Turkish descent and having lived all over Europe, she cooks healthy delicious international food. For the start of Restaurant Row, she prepared a samosa-style snack stuffed with different vegetables and accompanied by a dipping sauce. The wooden picnic table was full of assorted drinks: champagne and crème de cassis for Kir Royales, wines, porto blanc, and fresh juices for those that wanted non-alcoholic drinks. Time slowed down as we began to relax and savor the evening. To everyone's surprise, the kazoo orchestra stood and started off the evening with "Food, Glorious Food!"

Next stop, Ann and Peter's for the entrée. Each house was marked with a small lantern lit by a single candle. We happily sauntered up the street, wine glasses in hand. Inside the silk and painting studio where they work was a large table beautifully set with white square dishes on Ann's Friendship tablecloth. Each of us signed the cloth in ink, and later, Ann would embroider each signature in colorful thread. On vintage china platters were Peter's homemade wheat bread spread with black olive tapenade and a roasted cherry tomato. As we passed the plate around, Ann delivered small bowls of fresh pasta topped with Peter's homemade pesto from basil grown in our garden. Delicious!

After a brief stomach-resting period and a kazoo performance of "Volare," we walked down the street and into La Cascade's candlelit dining room. The table was set with a beautiful woven Provençal tablecloth and colorful ceramic plates from a local potter. Gwen, the owner and creator of La Cascade, and our good friend Leo prepared the main course. A gorgeous Chicken Marbella along with couscous and roasted red peppers, served family style. We needed a bit of time to rest and make room for more food, luckily supplied by the infamous kazoo orchestra! "Quizas" ("Perhaps, perhaps, perhaps").

Next stop was Christopher and Bill's. They are our best friends from California who were renting a house on our street for two weeks. Both have spent time in Durfort and know all of our friends. They had just arrived that afternoon after a long flight, so we gave them the easy course—cheese! As we gathered in their salon, the aroma of fresh and aged cheeses started to fill the room. Lovely French cheeses like Boursault, smoked Gouda, Swiss Bergerie, and aged Comté, along with little disks of local goat cheese, green and dark purple grapes, and fresh bread. My fave was a creamy Reblochon oozing out and sliding off my slice of bread. Well, it was hard to find a song about cheese, so we played "Wilkommen" (Welcome) from *Cabaret*.

Last stop of the night—our house, out in the garden along the flowing river, the table lit with all the candles I could find. We fell into chairs, happy and relaxed, and only one more course to go! I made an almond tart with fresh raspberries, cherries, blackberries, and red groseilles, and we finished off with coffee or mint tea, chocolate and Frangelico (hazelnut liqueur) or mint Get. Get is a peppermint-flavored liqueur that Revel is known for. The distillery was founded in Revel in 1787 by two brothers.

A perfect magical evening. We sat by the river enjoying each other's company. No dancing that night; we were all too full of food and wine, but our kazoo orchestra was in full swing, ending with "I Like Coffee, I Like Tea."

GOING CRAZY? THE VENT D'AUTAN

Just like Provence has their Mistral winds, we have our version called the *Vent d'Autan*. The word *Autan* comes from the old Provençal *auta*, which comes from Latin *altanus*, which means "wind of the high seas." According to the ancients, the wind of Autan blows one, three, or six days, then brings rain. It is usually a warm wind but depends on the temperature of the Mediterranean Sea. The average speed is 18–25 mph but can gust up to 75 mph, which was recorded in Toulouse in 2012! It can take off roof tiles, uproot small trees, and toss aside anything that isn't tied down; our patio umbrella once landed several houses down.

In our village, many old-timers can predict the length of the wind from the first day. I'm not sure how they do this—apparently a magical secret—but I always go seek out Roger to find out how long this incessant wind will last.

It is said to cause people to go mad. A famous saying translates as "When the Autan blows, the madmen of Albi dance." Actually, as far-fetched as that sounds, I can understand. Last summer we had one that raged for six days. Never stopped. Not for a minute. The windows and doors in our sixteenth-century house rattled and shook all day and all night. Loose shutters on street houses banged incessantly all through the day and night. Leaves blew into our house from places that we could not see. It was impossible to sleep—there was a constant low roar. Walking down our cobblestone streets became a challenge as you literally could be tipped over. I could not focus or think clearly. Everyone we ran into was irritable and grumpy. And though I did not lose my mind, it certainly was a challenge! Then on day seven, just all of a sudden, an immediate full stop. Just stopped. Calm. Perfectly quiet. Ah, sweet relief.

THE DURFORT STREET CINEMA

Our village is "famous" for our Street Sheet Cinema Nights. During the summer, when there is no Vent d'Autan, we schedule several cinema nights. It started with Leo, who was Assistant Dean of Animation at CalArts in Los Angeles. He surprised us all by showing the recent senior graduate films. He strung a large white sheet from one side of the street to the other, and everyone brought chairs, snacks, and wine to share. The next year we got fancier. Updated equipment run by Niall and Paul from the next street over allowed us to show DVDs. We have watched *Love and Mercy*, about the Beach Boys, and several other films throughout the years. These special nights are something our two streets really look forward to, and everyone in the village is invited. Young and old crowd together in plastic garden chairs, antique wooden chairs with beautiful caned seating, blankets, and plump pillows to lay on. Even an old easy chair is dragged out. Wine is kept cold in the little waterway that runs down the middle of the street, bowls of nuts and crackers are passed around along with cornichons (pickles), cheeses, sausage, and maybe even a pizza. Best movie nights ever!

SPECIAL BASTILLE DAY CELEBRATION

I had a lovely opportunity to share a great dinner and evening with friends in Castelnaudary—a town half an hour south of Durfort. Our American friends Roger and Cheryl have an apartment right on the Canal du Midi where the fireworks for Bastille Day take place. They spend half the year in France and half the year in Hawaii. It has been wonderful to connect with another American couple in France who like adventures like we do and are always ready to say yes to new experiences. Their apartment has an open kitchen and comfy living room with a huge picture window that looks out over the Canal du Midi. Luxury barges and small pleasure boats traverse this four-hundred-year-old canal that connects the Mediterranean to the Atlantic. And tonight the fireworks barge will be there!

As I entered their apartment the aroma of cassoulet cooking in the oven almost made me swoon. Cassoulet is our regional specialty, and the towns of Toulouse, Carcassonne, and Castelnaudary all claim to be where the dish originated, and each has a slightly different recipe. In my opinion, Castelnaudary is the home of the best cassoulet and hosts the official weeklong Cassoulet Festival. A true cassoulet is a forty-eight-hour process made in a handmade, sloped earthenware dish. Luckily for us, it's available as takeout from restaurants that specialize in making it.

Yummy Cassoulet

Roger brought the large dish to the center of the table. It's too heavy to pass around, so Roger served us all. He dipped the big spoon into the luxuriant stew, making sure we each got a piece of the special sausage, the melt-in-your-mouth duck confit, and the soft, creamy white beans (*haricots blancs*). The crispy topping is created not with breadcrumbs but by constantly turning the bottom crispy bits to the top over the forty-eight hours. It is truly one of the most delicious meals. But beware! Do not eat anything at all the twelve hours before—it is impossible to stop eating it before it hits the stomach with a heavy thud.

At 10:00 p.m., we rolled ourselves from dining room chairs to the glass window. It was almost time for the fireworks to begin. I have never in my life had such an unusual fireworks experience. We were safely behind the glass, but the fireworks were shooting right over us! Every time a new one went up we felt like we were right inside of the sparkling, dazzling display. The canal water luminously reflected the sky trails of the rockets and the twinkling bursts above us. As the lights showered down around us, we lifted our glasses in a toast to good friends and a truly unique experience.

COUNTRY WESTERN DAYS

In 2019 our village had its first annual Country Western Days. Strange but true! The Red Riders Dance Club from Revel, at least forty people, came for two days and danced ceaselessly from 4:00 p.m. Saturday till 1:00 a.m., and also all day Sunday. This group specializes in line dancing, and they were so amazing it made me want to join them the next year. It's a little disconcerting at first to hear country music sung with a French accent and also to see the sea of cowboy hats and boots and frilly dresses made of gingham. But you've gotta admire their passion for the genre. There are country western festivals all over France, including one about forty minutes from us. It lasts several days, and the celebrity guest of honor a couple years ago was Patrick Duffy from Dallas! Say what!

FÊTE DE LA MUSIQUE

The national *Fête de la Musique* (Music Festival) always takes place in France on June 21st. This celebration of making music encourages everyone, amateurs and professionals, to play music outside in their neighborhood streets, in the village centers, parks, and cafés. Larger towns and cities organize concerts where professional musicians play for fun and not for payment.

In October 1981, Maurice Fleuret, Director of Music and Dance at the Ministry of Culture, discovered in a study that one young person out of two in France plays a musical instrument. Thus began his dream of a way to bring people out on the streets to make music. The Fête de la Musique first took place in Paris in 1982.

We have our own Fête de la Musique here in our small village. One year we, both French and English speakers, gathered outside on our street. Nese, the chef at La Cascade, wheeled down a cart filled with wine, beer, and snacks for an impromptu musical apéro. The older residents peeked out of their windows to see what on earth was going on and slowly, shyly joined us on the street. We started with a French standard, *"La Vie en Rose,"* and soon the older residents were sharing beautiful country songs they had grown up with. The evening ended with us all raising our glasses and bottles while singing "Ninety-Nine Bottles of Beer on the Wall" in French and English. Same tune, different words, but same idea!

Another year, our friends Ann and Peter organized a group of friends outside their front door. The mint-green-trimmed door and shutters and Ann's climbing blue morning glories framed the musical combo. Ann played her guitar, Peter played the old keyboard he had brought from England, Kate played the flute, Jerry played his bass, and Ian expertly played the spoons. Friends and neighbors slowly filtered down the street to gather in a big semicircle around the group of musicians and joined in with song.

The larger town near us, Revel, organized a great evening with professional bands playing all over the town. A group of us wandered from street to street, square to square, fountains to cafés, listening and dancing to rock and roll, classic French songs, salsa, rap—everything. I asked Peter to join me in a cha-cha. In between songs we sat and enjoyed a glass of wine and kept going well past midnight.

COPPER CITY FESTIVAL

For several years our little village had a fabulous festival called Copper City. The festival was a combination of a few odd events. First of all, the music was rockabilly, with three music groups on Friday night and three on Saturday night. There was lots of fast dancing—as soon as the crowd got warmed up and had enough wine. The festival also featured a classic car exhibition including an American pink Thunderbird from the 1950s. And to top it off, a gathering of motorcycle clubs—at least a hundred motorcycles and cyclists of all ages. The Sons of Anarchy arrived in our sweet little village. It was a bit strange and confusing at first to see hundreds of leather-clad bikers among our old medieval village. But unlike the TV show, there was no drama at all. They came to our sweet café, shopped the copper shops, and enjoyed the fresh, cool water from our magic fountain. Many camped in tents on the green lawn surrounding our tourist car park and set up artisan booths featuring anything you might want or need for your cycling life: helmets, t-shirts, bandannas, lots of leather vests, and cool jewelry. Amazing!

On Sunday morning Dan and I rushed down to the car park to experience the *ballade*—though we didn't know what that was. A ballade is a slow drive, at about 30 mph, through the countryside and the small villages to show off the cycles and vintage cars. On cue at 11:00 a.m. all the motorcycles and cars revved up dramatically for several seconds and took off in a long promenade for the next couple of hours. They wound their way through the small villages that dot the countryside here and then circled back to Durfort for one final gathering before packing up and moving off to their next rendezvous. I hope they will return next year.

FESTIVAL COMMITTEE MEETINGS

We want very much to be a part of our village, so even though we do not speak much French, we often volunteer to be on different festival committees. These meetings are a village experience not to be missed.

Last spring Dan and I arrived at the mayor's house at 8:00 p.m. We were very curious to see inside his house, as it is one of the oldest in the village—over five hundred years old. We knocked on the ancient door, and as we climbed the stairs to the second floor, we were astounded to see beautiful African artwork on all the walls. Our mayor also owns a pharmacy in Revel and actively raises funds for his charity in Senegal. He's been collecting paintings, sculptures, rugs, and other beauties during annual visits there.

A fire was slowly burning in the big hearth (these old houses can still be cold in springtime), and the long rustic farm table was set for fifteen. Our fellow villagers drifted in over the next thirty minutes, and the table was laden with yummy dishes that each of us had brought to share. This potluck is called, for some reason, an *auberge Espagnole*, which strangely translates as "Spanish hotel." Hm? There were many pizza variations (my three-in-one sheetpan pizza was a hit), homemade savory and sweet tarts, salads, beautiful cheeses and sausages, fresh fruit, and bottles and bottles of wine—all three colors—white, rosé, and red.

Dan and I circulated, trying out our limited French with a bit of Franglais and pantomime to boot. *"Ca va?"* (How's it going?) The reply is the same: *"Ca va! Merci!"* (Fine! Thank you!) Good, we'd got our opening greeting down.

About 9:00 p.m. we all sat down to drink and eat. Dan and I thought to ourselves, *Gosh, when does this meeting begin? We will be here until midnight.* But food and wine are always first on the list at these village business gatherings. And so, we happily passed each dish around for all to share. At that point, the dense chatter among everyone was just a buzz of indecipherable French to my ears. We smiled and went with the flow as best we could. Finally, the meeting was called to order by our chairperson. And the grand debates began!

I think there's nothing a French person likes better than a good debate.

Anna said, "How much will we charge for the festival dinner?"

Bernard offered up, "Let's make it inexpensive. Eight euros."

Olivier countered with, "No, must be more—twelve euros!"

Jean Claude said, "Fifteen euros, at least!"

Pascale, with a fist on the table, "No, there will be families. Six euros!"

These debates—whether it's about the poster design, how much to pay the festival chef, how much to charge for drinks, or where the rubber ducky fishing should take place—can go on for hours. And I do mean hours! We felt like ping-pong balls looking back and forth at each speaker, trying to understand rapid-fire French—even faster than usual, as emotions were running high. We literally only understood about 10 percent of what was said.

Once in a while, someone asked us *"Comprenez vous?"* (Do you understand?) Dan and I sadly and somewhat embarrassedly shook our heads no, and the mayor kindly gave us a two-second translation. At midnight, our brains fried, we were the first to depart. As we stood up to leave and say our goodbyes, Olivier said, "Even though you understand nothing, we are so happy to have you here."

And he meant it. They do understand that we are there to help in any way we can, and that is much appreciated on both sides.

TCHATCHASSON AND MY "I LOVE LUCY" MOMENT

Tchatchasson. Such a strange word, yes? This is the name of a festival that was in our village for three years in a row. It means celebrating the spoken word—as in storytelling, poetry, words set to music, and song. Starting at noon on the festival day, the best storytellers from our area led festival-goers to different spots in the village where they entranced young and old with fanciful stories. During the day there were workshops on writing and setting words to music. At 6:00 p.m., we gathered by our magic fountain for a poetry slam! Poets from the area hypnotized us with the spoken word, rhymes, and free verse. Even though I could not understand the language, I was moved by their passion and emotion.

At the first Tchatchasson, and when we were very new to the village, we decided to volunteer to help serve the village dinner for over a hundred people attending the festival. Long tables covered in colorful cloths were set up near the fountain for the dinner. We were told to report to the committee ladies who were plating the meal and serving it. We arrived, and they all looked rather shocked that their volunteers were three Americans and one English. Our first task was to prepare the starter salad. None of the ladies spoke English, and our French was very limited then. But they had prepared a salad model for us to follow. A bed of lettuce with four tomato quarters placed in a pinwheel, topped with roasted, chopped beets and a sprinkle of corn.

Dan was responsible for separating the thin plastic plates that were

"I Love Lucy" moment

almost fused together, and that started our backup woes. Niall laid on the bed of shredded lettuce and added the tomato pinwheel, then Susi the chopped beets, and me the sprinkle of corn. I also had to carry the finished plates to a table behind me. So, off we went. Though we were working as fast as we could, we soon had a backup—a traffic jam of plates piling up. I felt like I was having an *"I Love Lucy"* chocolate factory moment. We grabbed, sprinkled, and grabbed again. I sprinkled as fast as I could, but at about plate eighty I realized I was running out of corn—I had been sprinkling too much. No way was I going to tell the stern committee ladies, so whenever their backs were turned, I scooped up corn from the plates that were already made and added to the new plates. And we finally made a hundred and twenty plates! We were each given a large glass of wine, and toasts and laughter followed.

At 10:00 p.m. the performance art event began in the performance space on the top floor of the Triple Zero factory here in town. Triple Zero produces high-end arctic gear as well as duvets and pillows—anything made with a high-quality goose down. This large space is set up to show films or host performers and is filled with comfy sofas and chairs. That night the stage was covered with about two inches of beautiful down feathers from the factory. A man quietly entered and slowly began turning in a circle, arms outstretched, sometimes reaching to the heavens. He closed his eyes, and as he whirled faster and faster he went into a trance. As he twirled, the feathers started slowly to lift and spin and rise and fall and whirl in gorgeous circles—we were under a spell. An exquisite moment to end a special festival day.

LA FÊTE DE L'EAU

This past Sunday our village had the fourth annual *Fête de l'Eau* (Water Festival). Water has been very important to this village from the thirteenth century on. There is the River Sor, which runs alongside the village and at one time had fourteen copper ateliers along it. The huge pistons that shaped the copper bowls were driven by large wooden water wheels. Unique to our village are the small waterways running down the three village streets—they served as part of the process in the copper ateliers that lined these streets (now houses!).

We hung hundreds of brightly colored triangular flags crisscrossing the streets and around the village square. We made a beach! *Le Durfort Plage* had its own cabana, boat, sand to play in, and beachwear accessories to take photos with. All day long, wonderful activities for young and old. This year I ran the Traveling Art Rocks booth for kids. I had hundreds of flat rocks that were collected by friends. On the back of each rock, I printed *Durfort 2021*. The kids (and adults too!) painted designs on the front of the rocks, then took the rocks with them to place somewhere else—maybe their own village or somewhere they will travel to in the future. Then another person somewhere on the planet will pick up their rock, see where it originated, and move it somewhere else. There is a Facebook group for Traveling Art Rocks to track your rock!

Dan was in charge of a new booth, the Sardine Can Fishing Booth. He worked for days on magnetizing the cans along with a magnet at the end of the fishing line. I have to say it was fraught with problems right up until the morning of the festival. But, happily, it turned out to be the most successful and popular booth! Other villagers helped

The Fete de L'eau boat race

kids to build boats out of recycled materials for a boat race down the street waterways in our village.

The highlight of the day was a waiter relay obstacle race—holding a tray of plastic tumblers filled with water, players had to navigate through the streets of the village, spilling as little as possible. The teams were made up of all ages and were cheered on enthusiastically. Trout fishing, storytelling, creating flower art in the river, a water slide, rubber ducky fishing, and

The waiter relay race

My red-haired mermaid debut

a show of water art at our village gallery all contributed to a great day in our village. I sang in the Fête de l'Eau choir in our small, sweet church. The acoustics there make an average choir sound fantastic—we sang water songs in French and English ("Singing in the Rain" and "Raindrops Keep Falling on my Head"). The day ended with an apéro for all and a potluck dinner in the street. The French definitely know how to relax, enjoy, and savor sweet moments like this.

A SCARECROW CONTEST

One sunny day I got a call from my arty friend Vero to come down to her Moulin du Chapitre B&B and meet with her arty friends for a special project. I arrived a bit late, and the group was already hard at work designing scarecrows for the Soreze scarecrow contest (*Épouvantail* in French).

We were partnered up in teams of two. Vero and her friend Bibi were making a ten-foot-tall scarecrow with a gown of used

Winner of the Scarecrow contest

silver compact discs, a bicycle wheel for the head, and finished off with knee-high olive-green rubber wader boots! Josie and Marie were making a very tall—at least twelve feet—elegant lady in white, her gown made out of yards and yards of white strapping tape, and she was holding a white umbrella. Her long hair magically flowed out horizontally into the air.

My partner Britta had already started. She was creating a "sexy" scarecrow in a skimpy outfit. I didn't find it very appealing at all, but I was late and there to help, not complain. First off, I donated my lime green socks for her naked feet. Her head was a white Styrofoam wig head garishly made-up with big eyelashes, blue eyeshadow, and red pouty lips. We added a huge tangled mass of fine copper wire for hair, topped with an upside down basket filled with red and green Christmas lights. Hmm… I was a bit embarrassed.

Off we went to Soreze to deliver the scarecrows. The wader scarecrow was placed in a small pond on the grounds of the mayor's building. The elegant lady in white had a beautiful spot at the entrance to the grounds, welcoming everyone to the park. Our "sexy scary" lady was placed almost behind a bush, possibly signaling for someone to come join her? Over the next few days, votes were cast, and we were all called to the park for the prize-giving ceremony. The elegant lady in white won first prize. Not surprised—she was beautiful. Second prize went to Vero's silver CD-wading lady. And shock of all shocks, the third prize went to our sexy lady! The mayor called us up front to a round of applause and gifts and even a sendoff by the village brass band. What a day!

A TUPPERWARE PARTY, FRENCH STYLE

Well, in case you didn't know, Tupperware is international and universal! My friend Ann and I were invited to a French Tupperware party. Husbands were invited, too, as the men would be cooking a barbecue to enjoy after the presentation. I had just read in a French etiquette article that it was good manners to arrive at a French gathering fifteen to twenty minutes late. This gave the hostess the extra time she might need. So we decided that we should be twenty minutes late to the Tupperware party.

When we drove up we could see a group of men and a group of about eight women all looking at us—the Tupperware presenter had been waiting for us for twenty minutes! Oops—the first faux pas.

Since there was to be a barbecue, Ann and I did not eat dinner. The presentation started at about 7:30 p.m. Even though it was in French, I could tell by the gestures and the cadence and timbre of her voice exactly what the lady was saying. "And just for tonight…the special deal for you to buy…this, that, and whatever, is…" As nice as she was, she droned on and on. After an hour and half, Ann and I were shocked that we were instructed to migrate to the kitchen, where the presenter made two full recipes using two or three of the newest Tupperware items.

At this point it was after 10:00 p.m., and Ann and I were starving. Finally our hostess put out a spread of pizza and quiche. Ann and I looked at each other, shrugged, and said, "Well, I guess there is no barbecue, but thank goodness for this!"

We hungrily jammed pizza and quiche into our mouths. So, now feeling full and tired (it was getting on toward 11:00 p.m.) we made our way to the hostess to say thank you and take our leave.

"Oh no," she said, "the men are just getting ready to serve the barbecue—chicken, sausages, pork, and steak. And dessert too. You can't go yet!"

Ann and I looked at each other with horror. Finally, after restuffing ourselves on the meats and desserts we were able to escape the Tupperware party after midnight. We survived, but just barely, our first (and last) Tupperware party!

KARAOKE NIGHT AT THE CAFÉ

One summer our village café got a karaoke machine and designated Thursday night as karaoke night. Ann Mason and I wandered down to see if anyone showed up and see what was happening. There were a few villagers already there. Tall, distinguished Mr. Gagner, with a head of gorgeous white hair and a big barrel chest, was dressed in a suit as if he were going to the opera. Two of our fun-loving British friends were already deep into their red wine. Several French neighbors wandered in and took a seat, curious like us. In a small village like ours, a karaoke machine is a big event!

We all waited for someone to be the first to step up to the plate. It was Mr. Gagner of course. He had been ready to sing since he arrived. He signaled Elodie to start the music and began with "La Mer," a French song made famous by Charles Trenet. With great emotion and dramatic sweeps of the arm, he absolutely enjoyed himself. We all clapped enthusiastically. He signaled Elodie again for this next selection, and his next and his next—he would not stop. He's an imposing man in the village with a stern glare, and Elodie was at a loss as to what to do. He had a good voice, but really! As the applause became quieter and quieter, he got the message and took a seat. Now who's next?

After a glass of wine (and enough of Mr. Gagner) Ann and I took a look at the songbook. It was filled mostly with French songs that we didn't know, but then we spied "La Vie en Rose," and with a little encouragement from our friends, we headed to the front of the bar. Ann has a decent voice and mine is okay, so we barreled on through. No one else made a move to get up, so next up was Lesley and me—we found the small section of English songs at the back of the book and chose, unfortunately, to tackle "Roxanne" by Sting. Oh my! We proceeded to murder it. And (what were we thinking?) followed up with Adele's "Rolling in the Deep." Talk about an embarrassing night! But everyone was in good humor and enthusiastically applauded anyone who had the guts to get up there!

RECIPES

Easy Breezy Company Salmon
Preheat oven to 400°F. Make a 1:1 mixture of brown sugar to whole grain mustard and mix completely. The amount will depend on how much salmon you are making. I usually start with a big tablespoon of each for two pieces of salmon filet. Sprinkle a bit of salt and pepper on the salmon. Place skin-side down on a lightly oiled, foil-covered dish. Slather on the mustard/brown sugar mixture on top of the salmon. Bake 12–15 min until salmon is done.

Parmesan Roasted Carrots
Preheat oven to 400°F. Line a baking sheet with foil and spray on a little olive oil. Put ¼ cup olive oil, 2 tsp. minced garlic, 3 Tbsp. grated parmesan cheese, 2 Tbsp. Panko breadcrumbs, ½ tsp. salt and ¼ tsp. pepper in a large plastic baggie. Add 4–5 cups carrots, either baby carrots or large carrots that you have cut up into chunks. Shake shake shake. Spread out onto baking pan and bake 20–25 minutes until carrots are tender. Toss every now and then while baking. Serve hot.

ALMOND AND THREE BERRY TART

Preheat oven to 350°F. Put your pastry shell or pie crust in a tart or pie pan and prick the bottom with a fork. Mix 2 eggs with ½ cup of sugar, 1 cup of almond powder, a pinch of salt and ⅓ cup melted butter. Pour this into the bottom of the tart pastry. Then spread 2 cups of fresh fruit on top, for instance, a blend of strawberries, raspberries, and blueberries. Bake 30–35 minutes.

THREE-IN-ONE SHEETPAN PIZZA

I make this with store-bought pizza crust in the United States, or you can make your own. In France I get the ready-made pizza pastry from the grocery store.

Preheat the oven to 375°F. Place the pastry on a sheet of parchment paper in a 9x13 inch pan.

For eggplant section: Cut 1 eggplant into slices and roast or saute until browned. Chop onions and 1 garlic clove and sauté in olive oil till translucent. Add a little oregano.

For zucchini section: cut zucchini into rounds.

For red pepper section: Sauté 1 chopped red pepper and 1 chopped small onion until translucent. Add rounds of merguez sausage (or sausage of your choice) and sauté till browned.

To make the pizza: Mix 2 packages of softened Boursin cheese and ¼ cup sour cream. Spread on top of pizza crust. On the first third of the pizza, spread out sautéed onion mixture and top with eggplant slices. On the middle third, overlap slightly the zucchini slices. Sprinkle with olive oil, salt, and pepper. On the last third, spread on the red pepper, onion, sausage mix.

Cover the whole pizza with a heavy sprinkle of shredded parmesan cheese. Bake for approximately 30 minutes till pizza crust is golden brown and cheese is bubbling.

5.
Exploring the Lauragais

Lac du Saint Ferreol

OUR REGION IN SOUTHWEST FRANCE is still relatively undiscovered and still authentically French. Although we're only an
hour from a big city, Toulouse, being way out in the countryside
allows for special trips to small undiscovered places. Just a short
drive away are unusual places unique to our region, the Lauragais.
Come with me and explore the lakes, Roman ruins, museums,
and festivals within a short drive of Durfort.

DINNER AT THE LAKE

Lac du Saint Ferreol is less than a ten-minute drive from our
village. The steep winding road up the Montagne Noire to the
lake is always a part of the Tour de France when they come to

our area. The cyclists either have to slowly trudge up the steep winding road or have the excitement of speeding down the road, leaning right and left at the tight hairpin curves, and then finally sharply turning the corner at the bottom to head straight into Revel's central square. The lake was created as an integral part of the Canal du Midi, the waterway that connects the Mediterranean to the Atlantic Ocean. Pierre-Paul Riquet was the engineer responsible for the construction of the canal, which started in 1666. Riquet needed to provide a sufficient water reservoir, this lake, to allow the many locks to function year-round, even in the dry summer season. The canal, completed in 1681, is a UNESCO World Heritage site and one of the oldest canals.

The lake is beautiful, with beaches, swimming areas, tennis courts, climbing walls, pedal boats, catamarans, kayaks, wind-surfing, picnic spots—it's all here. Along two sides of the lake are several restaurants and cafés, cottages, and hotels; it's a busy summertime resort center. We always go soon after we arrive in Durfort to celebrate the beginning of summer. There is a quiet, shaded walking path on top of the dam and around the whole lake that takes about an hour to complete. We like to walk the route and then settle in for a nice carafe of wine and dinner. Our favorite restaurant is Renaissance du Lac.

There are many regional specialties on the menu, but we get stuck on two of our favorites. The chorizo and merguez (spicy lamb sausage) pizza and the delicious salad (that I can't get enough of) called *tipasto spaccanapoli*. It's layered stacks of roasted red peppers, eggplant, zucchini, and tomatoes interspersed with smears of pesto and slices of parmesan. In the center of the five veggie stacks is a lovely green salad and crisp breadsticks. I've created my own version to share with you, and the recipe is at the end of this chapter.

BERNIQUAUT ROMAN RUINS AND SOREZE

Berniquaut is an archaeological site high on the hill in between our neighbor village of Soreze and our village, Durfort. It has been inhabited since prehistoric times, over thirty thousand years ago. It was the site of a farming community during Roman times and was settled high on the mountain top because it was a natural defensive place. Several Roman ruins are being excavated each year—more than a hundred lodges, meaning there were several hundred inhabitants here. Eventually, the inhabitants left this high spot (it was completely deserted by the thirteenth century) and resettled in the lower villages of Soreze and Durfort.

It's a moderate hike up to Berniquaut from our village. The graceful uphill walk on a gravel trail of shaded switchbacks takes about an hour. At the top you have glorious views looking down on Durfort—we can even spot our house! Dan and I took a picnic lunch and sat high on the top of the mountain under trees, enjoying sandwiches of sharp Pyrenees cheese, *moutarde* potato chips (mustard flavor), and fresh tangerines, along with a slice of French strawberry cake I had made the day before.

You can explore the ruins, even walk on the stone foundations that have been uncovered. There are several information kiosks with pictures of what Berniquaut probably looked like when it was inhabited. A short walk from our picnic spot we can also look down on the village of Soreze. It's a charming medieval village with photo ops at every turn. Many of the houses are half-timbered with the second floor protruding way over the first floor by a couple of feet. One explanation for this was that taxes were based on the square footage of the ground floor—hence more space was gotten by building the upper floors "out."

The cultural center in Soreze is the Abbaye Ecole. This monumental building has a history dating back to AD 754 with the founding of a Benedictine abbey. In later years it served as a national military boarding school training many of Napoleon's generals. The military school closed in 1991 and was transformed into the cultural hub of Soreze. The former stables became individual galleries, book shops, and a tea house. The former school now houses the Dom Robert Tapestry Museum. Each year in July there is a three-week music and opera festival held in the large courtyard of the Abbaye Ecole called Festival de Musiques des Lumieres.

MUSÉE DOM ROBERT

The *Musée Dom Robert*, a new museum in Soreze, is devoted to the glorious tapestries of the Benedictine monk Dom Robert. He resided at the monastery En Calcat, fifteen minutes away from our village. This monastery, built in1890, is still a working monastery of fifty Benedictine monks. There are several services a day open to the public, including nightly vespers and a Sunday morning service with Gregorian chants.

Dom Robert spent ten years studying and creating his art in Aubusson, a center of tapestries. He then came to En Calcat in

1958, where he lived until his death at the age of ninety. This is where he created his masterpieces of tapestry art, and he is considered one of the most admired and masterful tapestry designers of the twentieth century.

This brand new, wondrous museum is five minutes from our village and features countless tapestries, along with his original drawings with the exact placement of each of the color yarns he used. When I first walked in, I was astounded by the vibrancy of his colors and how modern and current his art felt. Dom Robert focused all of his work on nature and specifically on the flora and fauna of our Montagne Noire: flowers, trees, foliage, horses, chickens, goats, sheep, bees, ducks. He said, "There is only one thing that is right, that is nature. Nature is real, real." Museum visitors can see these huge tapestries from many viewpoints: the ground floor looking up at the tall tapestries, and second-story landings looking down on the tapestries. As I wandered the museum I came upon his *Tree of Life* tapestry. Populated with blue flowers, fall foliage in oranges and earth tones, and wild feathered pheasants playfully cavorting on the branches, it took my breath away.

ISSEL MEDIEVAL FAIRE

In the small nearby village of Issel, there is an annual Medieval Faire that overtakes the village in June. This village of five hundred residents is laid out in a circle that spirals down from the top. Dan and I parked the car, climbed the hill, and entered the village through an ancient stone archway with the village crest on the keystone. Once past the entry, the inclined cobbled path leads to the ramparts of what was once a walled city with a glorious view to the south of the snowcapped Pyrenees, overlooking the fertile Lauragais fields of gold and green.

It feels similar to an American Renaissance fair, but there is a real air of authenticity here. Many of the townspeople dress up in medieval garb handed down from their ancestors, and you can experience a fairly authentic "day in the life" in the Middle Ages. Bagpipes play as you wind your way up through the village. Horses, soon to be in the jousting contest, are decked out with banners and armor. Over fifty craft and food vendors line the street, selling medieval jewelry, handmade knives, beautiful calligraphy, pots of homemade jam, and miniature paintings. We came across several village men dressed in chain mail, getting ready for the fight in the afternoon jousting competition. Accordionists and small brass bands played old French songs throughout the streets, and older couples danced ever-turning waltzes in the village square. A blacksmith showed us how he made horseshoes and a beautiful medieval hinge for a shutter. As I watched the falconer working with his falcon (with a wingspan of five feet), I thought how special it was to experience this day. It's a party that will go throughout the evening with stilt walkers, jugglers, and fire eaters, grilled sausages and frites, ending with a bonfire in the village square.

Local Medieval Faire

A VILLAGE OF BOOKS

Montolieu is a village forty-five minutes from us, high on the "over the mountain" road that leads from our village to Carcassone. It's the scenic back road up and over the Montagne Noire and through beautiful verdant forests and golden fields. We snake up the winding mountain road out of Durfort and finally arrive at the top of the mountain at the village of Les Cammaze. The village of Les Cammaze has a busy tea and ice cream shop, a gorgeous walk or bike ride along a canal, and a colorful pottery shop where you can purchase local handmade pottery and also the sturdy brown ceramic dishes used for cassoulet and other casseroles and tarts. I started collecting a pattern of French red poppies intertwined with black olives and dancing swirls and add a piece to my collection each summer.

Next along the mountain top route is Saissac, an old village with a twelfth-century château. It's partially in ruins but makes for a stunning photo op with the snow-covered Pyrenees in the background. The white Charolais cows graze lazily in the meadows on top of this plateau as we continue on our way. And finally, we come to Montolieu. This small colorful village has reinvented and made a name for itself as a Village of Books—*Village du Livres*. Shops, galleries, and restaurants line the three streets, with most of them dedicated to books. Old Books, new books, antique postcards and prints, every kind of printed matter and ephemera you can name from centuries ago through the present. It's a treasure trove of amazing literary finds to use in art projects or collect for a window into another time and place. There's a spot for a lovely lunch at a special restaurant there called Les Anges aux Plafond (Angels on the Ceiling).

MUSÉE DU BOIS

This museum in Revel may sound boring—the Museum of Wood—but it is surely not. Since the 1800s Revel has been a center of skilled woodworking, furniture making, and especially marquetry, and even today continues as the capital of artistic furniture. The *Musée du Bois* celebrates this history.

As I walked through the open glass doors, I went straight to the special exhibition space off to the left. This is where contemporary exhibits are held that feature wood in combination with ceramics, paintings, metal, and other mixed media. This time it was very special. In December 1999, a most unusual event happened at the Palace of Versailles. A hurricane blasted through with winds up to 130 mph, devastating the grounds and gardens. Ten thousand unique and rare species of trees were uprooted and knocked down on the ground, including two trees planted by Marie Antoinette and one by Napoleon. Fundraising and replanting began right away, and the wood from the downed trees was offered to a number of artists so they could create sculptures from the fallen trees. This exhibit was beautiful and very emotional. Each artist found a way to honor the wood within their very different styles.

As I left the exhibit I wandered once again to the permanent exhibit of the history of Revel's furniture making. The exhibits on marquetry are worth the small price of admission alone. Marquetry is thin sheets of colored wood, metal, mother of pearl, and shells that are cut into intricate designs and then inlaid into the flat surfaces of the furniture. My favorite has always been the tall desk, the top inlaid with a vase of roses, chrysanthemums, and lilies; the ivory blooms are offset by the golden earth tones of different woods as leaves and foliage. But that day I came across a new favorite. Another desk with gorgeous wide curved legs appliqued with golden sculptural vines and leaves. And the desktop was inlaid with marquetry of four cherubs lazily reading and playing musical instruments. Their chubby little bodies were wrapped around harps and stacks of books.

The third floor houses a library of wood samples from all around the world. As my museum walkabout was ending, I heard the sounds of jazz coming from a room I had never been in before. I followed the music through a side door and into a room that must have been the kitchen of the original house where the museum now resides. At the end of this room was a huge hearth, and inside the hearth was Daniel Lucchese—a local jazz pianist and singer. Daniel had his piano and several percussion instruments (made out of wood of course) set up inside the hearth! It made a small, charming proscenium-style stage, and the acoustics were great. All this and a glass of champagne for the admission price to the musée. Come visit!

THE GORGEOUS REVEL FABRIC STORE

In the town of Revel, ten minutes from us, is a lovely *les tissus* (fabric store) right off the main square. It was owned by Madame Lopez, a chic older woman whom I met through Gwen Gibson. Since my workshops at La Cascade included making a fabric-covered book, I thought it would make a great field trip to take the workshop gals to Madame Lopez's fabric store. Gwen and I went beforehand to investigate and ask if it would be okay to bring ten eager, enthusiastic ladies into her shop.

Madame Lopez, a woman of a certain age, always wore her hair in a high French twist and dressed in what looked to me like a Chanel suit. Her makeup was perfect, her neck adorned with a small string of pearls, tiny pearls dropped from her ears—she was lovely and a bit intimidating at the same time. Gwen introduced me and we smiled and shook hands politely.

Gwen and I were immediately entranced and seduced by the gorgeous bolts of fabric. Cottons, velvets, woven tapestries, organzas, nubby wools, exquisite hand-painted silks, on and on. Right away we spotted a big box of remnants called *coupons*. Without even thinking of our manners, we dropped to the floor and dug through the box with wild abandon. I looked over and spotted Madame Lopez a few feet from us. She looked startled at our enthusiasm, but she didn't look upset. We were so happy and excited to see small pieces of these beautiful fabrics—big enough for book covers and at such a low price of one to two euros. From that rendezvous on we three were great friends. Every time I brought my art groups there we were greeted by Madame Lopez, and the students were as excited as we had been on our first visit. Beautiful pieces of fabric the same size as the American "fat quarter" were bought, and the coupon box of remnants was always a favorite to hunt through.

LE TOUR DE FRANCE

Revel, the market town ten minutes from us, has played host to the Tour de France three times over the last ten years. Dan and I were stoked to be there for this event. We were told to get to the side of the road early, as the crowd would fill the area in no time. About six hours ahead of the estimated arrival we brought our chairs to the main road leading from our village to Revel, where the race was to end that night. The bikers would be racing downhill from the lake and making a hard left turn to go into Revel. We decided to plop ourselves there. Surely they would have to slow down here to make that turn, and that would allow me to get some great pictures!

The Tour de France

Being at the tour ahead of the racers is like being at a fun, weird festival with lots of music and singing and cheering and happy excitement. Decorated cars and motorcycles ride by, advertising the sponsors of the tour. The official Tour de France mini-truck comes by tooting a circus horn and stops to sell the official products: T-shirts, posters, umbrellas, noisemakers, lots of fun stuff. You know it's getting serious when the gendarmes ride by in marked cars. They are shortly followed by the press and photographers seated backward on motorcycles to catch the best pictures.

Then the excitement begins. First were the six at the front of the pack, including Lance Armstrong! They were gone in a flash—truly, a snap of the fingers. They did not slow down one second on the curve. As they made the sharp turn, their bicycles were almost horizontal to the ground. I could not get one picture. Just gone in a blur. The peloton followed—this is the group of up to a couple hundred riders all juggling for their space. I put my camera up and just started clicking furiously. Hardly slowing down at the curve, they were also gone in a flash. I did get a few good pics, though. There were a few stragglers

Fun at the Tour de France

as the day went on, but even though the exciting part of the race was over within a few minutes, it was still an amazing and joyful communal event.

SUMMER FUN

Summer is the time of year when there are *beaucoup, beaucoup* festivals of music, dance, and theater in southern France. And most of them are free to the public, sponsored by the French government and the regional departments. And boy, do they do it well! On any given night, there are several events to choose from within an hour's drive. The level of artistry—whether it be classical, jazz, pop, opera, theater, or dance—is very high. The French believe that the arts belong to the whole nation, and even the remotest villages have talented performers come to perform.

Carcassonne is the last remaining double-walled citadel in Europe and is an hour from our home. There are fifty-two towers along the circular outer ramparts, and it truly looks like the fairy tale castle village you picture in your mind. It has remained a popular village from the 1100s onward. Go early in the morning or at dusk and you can feel the magic of this beautifully unique village high on a hill. Wander the maze-like cobblestone streets, explore the château and cathedral, and enjoy the many shops and restaurants.

The summer cultural event here is the three-week-long Festival de Carcassonne. I always look for favorite American and European performers in music, dance, and theater: Sting, John Legend, Francis Cabrel, Patrick Bruel, and many others have performed here. After a dinner of cassoulet under the shady plane trees in the square, we walked to the amphitheater near the château to see the Bejart Ballet from Lausanne. It was a magical experience. The backdrop was the ancient stone walls surrounding the castle. The sun set with an orange sky that backlit the dancers as theater lights slowly came on. The dancers were magnificent, and I saw the most intense performance of Stravinsky's Rite of Spring ballet that I have ever seen.

Another special event we love is the Rio Loco in Toulouse. Each June at Rio Loco, a country is chosen and their culture celebrated with a four-day festival. In the big park in Toulouse, Les Prairie des Filtres, three soundstages are set up for ongoing music all day and evening and into the wee hours of the morning. There are exhibitions of arts and crafts, food booths featuring the country's specialties, and music, music, music. You pay a flat fee of five euros per day or fifteen for the whole event! Amazing.

Our favorite so far was the celebration of Algeria and Tunisia. We stopped first to fuel up with a spicy Tunisian chickpea soup. Then strolled over to one of the music stages featuring Rai. The Rai music was new to us and emotionally moving. Rai was first created in the 1920s as Algerian folk music that was especially popular with the poor and younger people. Rai, which translates to "opinion," is not afraid to focus on social, economic, religious, and political issues. The soulful lyrics are set against the beat of drums with flutes, trumpets, saxophones, accordions, and even electric guitars! Local folk music traditions blend with an underbeat of contemporary rock, jazz, and flamenco.

The audience that night was a true blend of all ages and nationalities, and we were all transfixed by the older Rai performers, now in their 70s, called The Legends of Rai. These men, all in beautiful pressed white linen suits, came onstage and gave the audience all their passion, hearts, and souls for their homeland. Young men sat on each other's shoulders, draped in their country's flag, singing along and reaching out to the singers with gestures of yearning and love. I had a huge appreciation for the passion these young people felt for their ancestral home.

THE TOULOUSE ANTIQUE FAIR

On the first Friday of every month there is an outdoor antique fair in Toulouse. Lucky for us it's only an hour's drive away. Or better yet, catch the bus from Revel to Toulouse for two euros and just enjoy the ride through the beautiful countryside. The bus lets you off right there at the fair.

It's time for an adventure! Dan and I caught the early bus at 7:00 a.m. and were at the fair in Toulouse by 8:15. First thing we noticed after disembarking from the bus was a delicious-looking patisserie, so of course we got a pain au chocolat to have with coffee at the fair. Many vendors were still setting up so we walked the show once, then stopped at the fair's café for a *noisette* with our pain au chocolat. A noisette is a small coffee (espresso size) with a dash of milk. Good fuel for circling the fair again!

These vendors, unlike the vide grenier vendors, are professional vintage dealers. They specialize in items from the 1800s through midcentury 1950s. I'm drawn to the white linen dishtowels with the iconic red stripes. Some are even monogrammed with the original owner's initials. And I jump for joy when I spot an antique door knocker. It's similar to the original one on our house from the 1500s. But this one I can take back to the US. It's in the shape of a curled hand wrapped around a plump apple, and the mustard-colored paint is partially peeling off to show the patinaed rusted iron. It's gorgeous and authentic, and these are very hard to find. I can't believe my luck. We also come upon a strange Napoleon-era costume on a mannequin, complete with red sash and two-cornered hat. One booth is filled with large vintage posters from Paris nightclubs.

Before hopping the bus back to our village we enjoyed the wonderful indoor food market in Toulouse—the *Marché Victor Hugo*. It has been going on since 1896! There is everything you can think of there and all displayed beautifully, from fresh oysters to enjoy with a glass of white wine, to hundreds of French cheeses and stacks of fresh produce. We came upon a booth with a fig and Gorgonzola pizza and had to have a slice.

Toulouse has so many places to enjoy—a grand cathedral, St. Sernin, and one of my favorite museums, Musée des Augustins. Also a contemporary art museum, Les Abbatoirs, and many, many other museums and galleries. The central plaza, *le capitole*, is always bustling with markets and concerts. And Toulouse is also where you can find great Indian food!

EARLY MORNING AT THE BAKERY

For three years in a row, Nese, the La Cascade chef, and I taught a weeklong Art and Cooking workshop. For the art part, we made a journal book from scratch to take notes in, along with pockets to stuff with recipe cards, ephemera from our field trips, and any other inspiration found during the week. Each day we also had a cooking class with Nese, which culminated in either our lunch or dinner for that day. Field trips included a tour and tasting at the local cheese maker, a wine tasting at a nearby château, farmer's market expeditions to buy incredible ingredients for class, and a *very* early morning day at the bakery.

Nese was able to convince a local baker to let us bring our group into the bakery to see what morning life is like there. Our group of ten arrived at 5:00 a.m., though the staff (the main baker and two assistants) had been there since 3:00 a.m. This bakery is known for making traditional baguettes along with an amazing daily assortment of specialty breads. We were given a demo of how baguettes are formed and baked. The space was small. We were constantly backing into corners to allow the bakers to do their dance: from the huge bags of flour, to the kneading tables, to the forming area where the traditional long shapes are rolled and laid into specially made curved bread pans, and finally to the ovens. Hundreds of baguettes were made for that day—for local restaurants as well as a long line of customers that snaked outside the door starting at 7:00 a.m. At the end of our time, we eagerly bought several loaves of bread—red pepper and garlic, walnut fig, apricot almond, Roquefort and chorizo, and one of my favorites, muesli bread made with an assortment of dried fruits and nuts. The morning inspired me to make a bacon and goat cheese quick bread. It was an eye-opening experience of the difficult life of a French baker. Our hardworking baker would return later in the afternoon to fire up their ovens for nightly specialty pizzas.

PIGEONNIERS AND GARGOYLES

Our rural area in France is known for the many exquisite *pigeonniers* dotting the countryside among the sunflowers, wheat, and poppy fields. Pigeonniers are large pigeon houses or dovecotes. Mostly round or square, and more rarely octagonal, they sit on four stone legs six to nine feet

A pigeonnier house

off the ground. The legs are topped with a mushroom-shaped cap to prevent unwanted animals from entering the main room of the pigeon house and eating the pigeons or their eggs. The large main room is typically made in the half-timbered style, wooden beams showing and spaces between filled with stone, brick, or mud. Tiled roofs are steep like a witch's hat, and the birds can easily enter and leave through small holes or windows in the roof or the walls. The inside walls are filled with nesting boxes where the pigeons will live with their mates for the rest of their lives.

Now let's talk about the size. These pigeonniers can be approximately 15x15 feet. They are large! And could house up to a thousand birds. Built between the thirteenth and nineteenth centuries, the possession of a pigeonnier was a symbol of wealth, status, and power. If you had one, you could eat meat every night if you wanted! Pigeons were highly valued for their meat and their droppings, which fertilized the fields. Their poop also contains one of the ingredients for gunpowder.

My first experience was at a bed and breakfast. We arrived in late afternoon, and the owner led us straight to a square pigeonnier! We cautiously climbed up the stairs (which had been added onto the outside), opened the door, and found a cozy little bedroom and bath for two. Our breakfast was served alfresco under our room between the four tall columns. It was a huge surprise when we found out that our neighbors in our village have one in their backyard. Robert converted the upstairs main room into his personal workout room and office. Down below, Annie made a wonderful summer kitchen with a huge cooking hearth and a large farm table to entertain family and friends.

During my art workshops, on our way back from Albi, we had the opportunity to stop at one for an up-close photo op. It's typical of our area and was built during the fourteenth century. I have a book that details, with a map and directions, all the many pigeonniers in our region of the Tarn. A day trip is in order to truly appreciate the elaborate and different styles of these large architectural wonders.

Another special architectural delight in our region is the many gargoyles. Close to us are numerous medieval churches that feature these unusual (and slightly alarming) sculptures. They are usually elongated fantastical animals built for two main purposes: to scare off evil spirits and to divert rainwater. The word gargoyle means "throat" in French, and the same word also describes the gur-

gling sound of water coming down a downspout. Gargoyles have a deep trench carved in the body, and the rainwater exits through the mouth. The gargoyles on the churches in Albi and Carcassonne are intense! The Musée des Augustins in Toulouse has a large selection that stand upright on the floor. Up close and personal, you can truly see the engineering and artistry of these wild creatures.

Carcassonne gargoyles

LES FANFARES

St. Felix de Lauragais is the small hilltop village known for their yearly street music festival called L'autan en Fanfare. It is also the home of our beloved friends, Claude and Marie, a couple in their eighties who have been together since they were thirteen years old! They are of French-Canadian nationality but have lived full-time in France for over thirty years. Lucky for us, that means they speak both French and English. Claude is an avid gardener and gourmet cook; Marie loves politics, knitting, and animals. They are funny and outrageous, generous, and they love to disagree with each other and then comically make up! Their walled village commands a view of the Montagne Noire and the snowcapped Pyrenees, along with five ancient windmill towers on the north and south sides.

Claude invited us to go to the fanfare with him and Marie. Fanfares are large brass bands, and the ones we have seen in France are outstanding—great musicianship but with a whack-a-doodle sense of humor. There are weird costumes and silly antics, and yet the music is highly professional. And so we arrived at the village square where already a competition of sorts was taking place between two bands. Musicians were decked out in leopard pants with pirate hats, long leather vests with feather boas, bright purple coats and tiaras. You can imagine, yes?

The master of ceremonies gave each band a challenge, and then the two bands competed for the best via audience applause. For instance, one band was given the task to create a song about cassoulet, one of the famous regional dishes here, and the other band had to make a song about Roquefort cheese. Each band (there were fifteen to twenty members in each) conferred for about a minute and then started playing and singing. Another challenge—fill the trumpets and trombones with water and play! What! It was a hoot. Weird, funny, and we all applauded wildly for our favorite.

Band players at Les Fanfares

WALKING WITH THE CAMINO DE SANTIAGO PILGRIMS

A few years ago Europe celebrated the four hundredth anniversary of St. Jacques, of the Camino de Santiago pilgrimage route fame. The long pilgrimage originates in several spots in Europe and ends at Santiago de Compostela in northwest Spain, where St. Jacques is said to be buried. This important pilgrimage has taken place since the ninth century. Although many associate this pilgrimage with religious or spiritual motivation, many participants make the journey for comradeship with other sojourners. Some close friends of mine

Entering Revel square with the Camino pilgrims

from Germany met and later married, having first met on the Compostela walk.

The anniversary organization held special events throughout Europe, and in our area there was the opportunity to walk with three pilgrims. The towns of Revel, Soreze, and the monastery of Encalcat are all along the pilgrimage route. Dan and I and two friends signed up for this special day. At 7:00 a.m. we met at the monastery to walk to Dourgne—about an hour's walk away or three minutes by car! We were led by the three official pilgrims carrying staffs decorated with silver *milagros*. Milagro means "miracle" in Spanish, and they are symbols of luck, good health, and hope for the journey.

There were about forty of us, including Mr. Calvet, a local historian, who was dressed in full medieval garb—a long blue linen robe trimmed in gold, a majestic hat, and a wooden staff adorned with a scallop shell. We were accompanied by three men on horseback in chain mail! Each pilgrim had an official Compostela passport to be stamped in each town they went through. In Dourgne, the mayor and townspeople greeted us with a breakfast spread of French pastries and fresh coffee.

Then onward to Soreze, about a two-hour walk (but only ten minutes by car). We weren't following the road, but hiking on the ancient route, which now goes through farmers' fields and rows and rows of sunflowers deep in bloom. Beautiful. At Soreze we were greeted by the mayor with a delicious lunch spread of ham and cheese sandwiches, fresh salads, and apple tart for dessert. Over lunch, we were given a short break, as the pace of this walk was *fast*. No stopping but for short water breaks along the way. From Soreze we walked to Revel, another three hours (five minutes by car). We were all getting a little tired by now—amazing to think what the three pilgrims had ahead of them. Weeks and weeks of more walking. We ended our eighteen-kilometer day there, ceremoniously marching into town, up and down the streets of Revel, where we were greeted with pomp and circumstance by the mayor and a brass band. We were escorted up the ancient bell tower to view the colorful houses from the 1300s that line the central square, and served a seven-course French dinner under the eaves of the fourteenth-century wood-covered market.

RECIPES

Layered Veggie Stacks

Preheat oven to 350°F. Make the sauce first: Heat 1 Tbsp. olive oil in fry pan. Sauté 1 Tbsp. chopped onion and 2 chopped garlic cloves until golden brown. Add 1 14-oz can crushed tomatoes, 2 Tbsp. tomato paste, ¼ cup white wine, 1 ½ tsp. balsamic vinegar, and a little salt and pepper. Simmer 20 minutes.

Whisk 2 eggs in a bowl. In separate bowl combine 2 cups breadcrumbs and 1 cup grated parmesan cheese. Cut 3 zucchini into ¾-inch rounds. Heat 2 Tbsp. olive oil in a pan. Dunk each round into eggs, then into breadcrumb mixture, then into sauté pan. Sauté both sides until golden brown. Drain on a paper towel.

In an 8x8-inch pan, make a bottom layer of the zucchini rounds, nestling them together. Then put a slice of pepperoni or chorizo on each, a bit of sauce, a handful of mozzarella and grated parmesan, and a basil leaf. Keep doing this till you have stacks, ending with zucchini and sauce. Bake at 350°F for 12 minutes. Add more cheese and bake for 5 minutes more.

Tunisian Chickpea Soup

In a large saucepan over medium heat, add 2 Tbsp. olive oil. Sauté 1 cup coarsely chopped onion for 5–7 minutes till golden brown. Stir in 4 cloves minced garlic. Cook for 1 minute. Add 1 Tbsp. of harissa or hot sauce of your choice. Stir in 1 15-ounce can chickpeas. Add 1 Tbsp. cumin and 1 Tbsp. salt. Add 2 cups chicken broth and 1 ½ Tbsp. lemon juice or vinegar. Simmer over low heat until onions have almost disintegrated. I like to add grilled sausage to this (sliced in rounds) and a few cut-up roasted potatoes. Add more chicken broth as needed.

Gorgonzola, Fig, and Pancetta Pizza

Preheat oven to 400°F. Buy or make a pizza crust. In a blender, purée 1 cup canned Italian tomatoes with a pinch of oregano and a little salt and pepper. Set aside.

Next, layer on top of pizza dough in this order: the sauce, shredded Italian four-cheese blend, 1 large plum tomato thinly sliced, a layer of pancetta or pepperoni, a sprinkling of gorgonzola cheese, 8 fresh figs quartered, and a drizzle of balsamic vinegar. Bake until crust is brown and toppings are bubbling.

Bacon, Zucchini, and Goat Cheese Quick Bread

Preheat oven to 350°F. Lightly oil a loaf pan. Cut ⅓ of a zucchini into rounds. Grate the rest of the zucchini. Lay it out on a paper towel and squeeze as much water out of the grated zucchini as you can. Sauté 12 strips of bacon and crumble into bits. Cut the goat cheese into bits to make ½ cup. In a bowl, mix 1 cup flour and 2 tsp. baking powder. In a separate bowl, mix together 3 eggs, 4 Tbsp. canola oil, ½ cup white wine, 1 tsp. chopped fresh thyme, and a little salt and pepper. Add the wet ingredients to the dry. Add in the grated zucchini, bacon bits, and goat cheese bits and mix. Pour into loaf pan. Place the zucchini rounds along the top of the loaf. Bake for 40–45 minutes.

6.
Beyond the Village

Gigantic Balloons for Albi Nuit Pastel

THE LANGUEDOC, OUR SOUTHWEST REGION of France, translates as the "Language of Yes." This inspires me to say yes to adventures and new experiences. From our village, we can easily be in the Pyrenees in one and a half hours, down to the Mediterranean in two hours, and into the heart of Provence in about three hours. Join me as we go a bit farther afield for more adventures.

CUQ EN TERRASSES

There is a very special restaurant-hotel about half an hour from our village. Cuq en Terrasses is owned by Andonis and Phillippe, and they have created an exquisite place to relax and eat divinely. The hotel and restaurant are located in a renovated eighteenth-century rectory right across from the beautiful old village church. They recently won an award from TripAdvisor: Second Best Small Hotel in France and Eleventh Best for Service among all the French hotels. (More than 16,000!)

I've had the good fortune to go for dinner every summer. The chef, Andonis, is a rotund Greek man. Whenever I spy him in the kitchen or during service, he always has a smile on his face. He finds what is in season and local to our area at the market and cooks up a five-course feast. On the grounds of Cuq en Terrasses are olive and fig trees, beehives, homegrown vegetables, and aromatic herbs, which make their way onto the nightly menus along with fresh local meats, fish, and, yes, wines! Phillipe welcomes and seats guests on the terrace overlooking the golden fields of the Lauragais and hands each guest the handprinted menu for the night. He is a thin Frenchman, more reserved in manner but always polite, with a subtle sparkle in his eye. Each year in their off-season they travel the world and find new inspiration and recipes.

The menu includes an amuse-bouche, an appetizer, main course, cheese plate, and dessert. This night was special. Along with our dear friends Christopher and Bill, we were celebrating two birthdays. First off—a drink to toast our birthdays! Every night of the week, besides a wine list, there is a special designer cocktail. Oh boy. Phillipe arrives with peach kirs for two of us and a special white foamy drink made with ginger beer for Dan and Bill. As we sat enjoying the setting sun over the vineyards, Phillipe arrived with our amuse-bouche, which translates as "to amuse the mouth." The cool cantaloupe-colored melon soup topped with a melon ball wrapped with a piece of ham surely whetted the appetite.

The French always allow for pauses between courses, not only to rest your stomach but to enjoy your surroundings and good conversation. As we chatted about our lives, the twinkling lights on the stone terrace slowly came on, and Phillpe stopped by to light the candles on our table and deliver the bright green fresh-grilled asparagus along with a creamy pale green asparagus flan.

Our main dish was inspired by their trip to Thailand— lovely rondelles of pork in a spicy Asian sauce, a small pile of perfectly cooked green beans, and a carrot-orange flan. Philippe stopped by often to offer fresh homemade bread. I had the lemon-dill bread.

After a shared cheese plate with five special French cheeses, my favorite course arrived. The smell of fresh cherries surrounded me. Deep red homemade cherry sorbet topped with a cherry *financier*. A financier is a small light and moist cake in a rectangular shape. The name is said to derive from the traditional rectangular mold, which resembles a bar of gold.

After dinner, Andonis came bounding out of the kitchen, sat down at their hundred-year-old pianola (player piano) in the dining room, and gathered us all together. Phillppe handed out thick songbooks and surprised us with his joyful harmonizing to Andonis's rich baritone. As Andonis "pedaled" the piano furiously, we spent the next half an hour singing and swaying enthusiastically to "Uptown Girl," two songs from *Les Mis,* and *"C'est si Bon,"* finishing up with a rousing tribute to Andonis's Greek heritage, "Never on Sunday." A truly memorable birthday!

BIOCYBELE

The French are on board with organic food, alternative energy, and alternative living styles. A little slower to the party than we were in the US, but finally the stores are getting larger sections of organic foods—called Bio in France.

We recently went to the Biocybele Festival, which happens once a year in the town of Grauhlet, about an hour from us. It's a two-day celebration of biodiversity, healthy lifestyles, alternative energy, and all things organic. It's a bit like walking back in time to the hippie era. Lots of long flowing hair and long flowing peasant dresses. Rows and rows of brightly colored festive booths selling organic fruit and vegetable plants and gorgeous flowers and herbs. Along with cheese, organic meats, fish, fresh breads, and patisseries are organic honey and hand-milled flours. You can also find organic oils and vinegars, organic beer and wine, and a large bookstore tent with everything you would want to know on gardening, agriculture, renewable energy, and sustainable lifestyles. We spot our favorite plant vendor and get our annual load of beautiful tomato plants along with lemon thyme, pepper plants, courgettes, white eggplants, and Thai and cinnamon basils. The festival is held each June—usually the first weekend.

THE POTTERY VILLAGE OF GIROUSSENS

In the *très petit* (tiny) village of Giroussens is a jewel of a museum, *Centre Ceramique de Giroussens* (the Museum of Contemporary Ceramics). This lovely village is close to Gaillac, which is the center of the wine-producing area closest to our village and about an hour away. I came upon this museum by chance in 2007 and make a point of visiting each summer. Each year the exhibitions have been outstanding. One side of the modern building is the current exhibition, featuring work by contemporary French potters. As I entered the exhibition room, I saw pedestals with ceramic teapots and teacups, the pedestal tops covered with overflowing milky tea! But wait, the milky tea had the same bright blue decorative patterns as that on the teapots. These ceramic interpretations of teapots and teacups, all oozing gracefully onto the pedestals, were playful and unusual. The other side of the building features a history of local and regional potters, including the sculptress and potter Mme. Lucie Bouniol, whose family home is right across the street. She lived from 1896–1988, received many art awards, and was a close friend of the writer Colette.

The village of Giroussens is filled with photo ops: old stone and timbered buildings covered with climbing roses, grape vines, and wisteria; the vineyards of Gaillac spill down the hills surrounding the village. As you enter the village church, it's like walking inside of a technicolor movie of Provençal fabric designs. Every piece of wall and ceiling is covered with intricate hand-painted designs in a riot of colors. I always finish my visit at L'echauguette, a lovely restaurant with a terrace overlooking the countryside. I had a simple and delicious salad of white beans, chorizo, and blue cheese (my version is at the end of the chapter).

NUIT PASTEL

We had crazy weather in the spring of 2019. Just when it finally seemed that "spring had sprung," another thunderstorm and days of rain came through. Our longtime residents here in the village said it was the wettest spring in twenty-five years!

But being forever hopeful, we decided to go to Albi for the *Nuit Pastel*. This is a yearly event in June, and we were excited to attend it for the first time. Starting at seven in the evening, several music groups perform in the old town, and you can wander from group to group all evening. Then at 11:15

The Albi Cathedral

p.m., there is a huge light and sound show at the cathedral in the central square with enormous artistic balloons: huge horses, kings and queens, medieval ladies waiting to be rescued by knights in shining armor, and dragons, all illuminated with multicolored lights and ready to float up high into the sky.

On our drive to Albi in the afternoon, a terrible storm rained down on us, but it lifted by the time we got there. The optimistic young woman at the tourist office assured us it was just temporary and things would be fine and go on as planned for the evening. We were early and decided to explore the area down by the River Tarn. As we wandered we came upon a little sign advertising a restaurant. Ready for an adventure, we found a hidden overgrown path and entered a magical bamboo forest. Tall shoots of dark green and ebony black bamboo surrounded small riverlets that fed into the main river. Stepping-stones in the river allowed us to keep going in search of this restaurant. Finally we came upon an old, weathered iron gate and the restaurant itself. There was a menu posted, and even though it was not open, it did not look deserted. Another time perhaps? We'll go!

Later we walked back up to the cathedral and stopped in one of the many brasseries on the central square for a bite to eat. Right across from us the music stages were being set up and the balloons were filling with air.

But then…dark and stormy clouds rolled in. At first everything continued on—musicians setting up, balloons blowing up and softly floating just inches above the ground. Over the next half an hour, though, the heavens thundered and the rain poured down in buckets. Musicians went running for cover using their music stands as umbrellas.

The balloons sat deflating sadly in the rain, and soon the main square was completely empty.

Oh, well. Hopefully next year!

APÉRO CONCERTS IN GAILLAC

Gaillac is the closest wine-producing area to our village—about forty-five minutes away. The vineyards were established during Roman times and are well-known for their vibrant red, white, and rosé wines. Every summer during July and August they offer apéro concerts on Friday nights. They take place in a lovely outdoor garden behind the former abbey that now houses the tourist office and the wine museum. Admission is only five euros! You are given tickets for a plate of sausage, cheese, chips, and two tickets for glasses of wine of your choice. There are usually six wineries to choose from. Tables and chairs surround a stage, and each Friday features a different type of music—salsa to traditional French music to rock to country! Soon after we arrived the band started playing, and couples and singles got up to groove to the music. Children joined in with abandon. Doesn't matter if you have rhythm or not, no one cares! After our wine (two glasses each), Dan and I got up the nerve to dance. We have our own style (cough, cough) but no one cares, and it is a great way to enjoy the freedom to just move to the music.

SHORT GETAWAYS TO ALBI, AN ARAB FÊTE, AND THE AMPHORALIS MUSEUM

A couple weeks ago we read about a tour of the new national theater in Albi where symphonies and operas are staged. It is quite impressive architecturally with a huge transparent "flying" window across the front of the theater. We thought it would be interesting and that we could possibly even get backstage. Little did we know that we were in for over two hours of tortuous, complicated, indecipherable, speed-dial French. I was feeling pretty positive that my comprehension of French had greatly improved over the last couple of years and felt I was up to the task of at least getting the gist of a lecture. Oh, *mon Dieu,* was I wrong. The lecture went on and on and was incomprehensible to me. It didn't help that the speakers were quite boring, with that tone of voice that is a universal drone. After two long hours, Dan and I could not escape fast enough.

Immediately we started a trek up and over the Montagne Noire to get to the *Occitane et Arabe* festival in Carcassonne. We had some trouble finding the somewhat obscure community center where it was taking place, so we stopped to ask for directions at a small *épicerie*. Within seconds there were four Frenchies, all with different opinions on where the place was and how to get there, trying to help us out. It was chaos! But all in good humor.

Finally, after zigzagging around Carcassonne for another half an hour, we arrived at this gathering of all ages to celebrate the music of Arabia and the old Occitan songs of the Languedoc. Occitan was the official language of the troubadours, who wrote poems and songs and frequently came to court to entertain royalty. It lost its favor among the nobility in 1539 when the king of France outlawed the language. Now there is a growing interest in keeping the language, songs, and poetry alive. This festival featured several music groups with a full slate of guitars, accordions, clarinets, violins, harmonicas, and fantastic singers.

The next day we were off again to the Amphoralis, a place I have wanted to visit for a long time. This is a museum that overlooks (literally sits above) the excavation site of large pottery workshops that existed only between the first to third centuries AD. Over seventy potter families lived here and mass-produced by hand the thousands of amphoras that were needed to ship wine all over the Roman Empire from the port of Narbonne about ten miles away. Fourteen large kilns, living spaces, and many amphorae have been excavated. You can learn about the daily life of the potters and even visit a garden with more than nine hundred plants that existed in the Gallo-Roman period.

CAMPING IN FRANCE

Ambialet is a tiny village about an hour and a half away. It is beautifully situated on a peninsula surrounded by a U-bend of the Tarn River. There is an old monastery and a Romanesque church that houses contemporary art exhibits, but the village highlight is the annual Blues Festival in June.

We dragged down our tent and sleeping bags from the attic, strapped our mountain bikes onto our little Citroen, and off we went to camp and attend the festival. Almost every town (and many villages) of any size has a campground—either a municipal campground or a private one. It's very popular in France to just take off and sleep under the stars. The French campgrounds are great. Most of them have grassy areas shaded by big trees, swimming pools, showers, and modern toilets (a personal requirement of mine), a café, small store, and sometimes even a restaurant with evening entertainment!

The campground at Ambialet is our favorite. Large trees shade plush, grassy grounds bordered by rose bushes. Two other couples joined us, and we had a grand time. One couple had turned their little white truck into a cool camping car. The other couple was trying out their new tent for the first time—we dubbed it the Palace, as it had a big, enclosed foyer/porch along with two separate rooms—all inside the tent! Ours was called the Doghouse, which is about the size of it, basically big enough for two sleeping bags and that is about it. Needless to say, I did not sleep great.

In the morning I got Dan's little camping stove started to make coffee and tea for our group. Walnut bread with butter and homemade jam, hardboiled eggs and fresh tomato slices, a cutting board of sliced cheese, and fresh strawberries—we had a delectable feast each morning. Then we were off on our bikes to explore the quiet, flat country lanes along the riverbanks. France is a cycling paradise because motorists are respectful of cyclists, especially in rural areas.

After a shower and nap, we were ready for dinner and music. The first night we shared a potluck at our campsite. I made my famous ratatouille crumble. Then into the village for music! It was a short ten-minute walk along the winding river from our campsite to the center of the village. The next night we ate at the festival—a great meal of *confit de canard* or Toulouse grilled sausages with fries. Yum! Six euros for food, and the music? FREE! Three bands were featured each night with music from 7:00 p.m. to 1:00 a.m. We loved the first group—a husband and wife, he on harmonica, she on a fiddle, singing soulful blues. As the night went on, the bands were bigger, the singing louder, and the crowd, fueled by food, wine, and a beautiful summer's night, happily danced the night away.

VACATION IN AVIGNON: A MIXED BAG

There's almost nothing more stressful than having car problems on a vacation in a foreign country where you do not have the necessary language skills—and on top of it all, the car breaks down on a Sunday! The story unfolds…

We had a great first day in a small village just northeast of Avignon, Villes sur Auzon, which has a yearly jazz festival. We attended the concert of the Michel Legrand Trio. He is a legendary musician and composer who wrote over two hundred film and television scores, in addition to many songs such as "Windmills of Your Mind," "Summer of '42," and the score and songs for *Umbrellas of Cherbourg*, one of my favorite films.

He was eighty-six then and seemed quite frail as he walked out to his piano with the help of the other two trio members. But then he sat down at the piano. There was a pause, and we all held our breath. With a burst of energy, his soul poured out his fingers and onto the keys. He transformed before my eyes into a young person, playing with a vitality that was awe-inspiring. He began each song with a melody that we recognized, but then soon he was off and running with incomparable improvisations leading us to outer space and beyond, and then finally returning home to the melody. A giant among jazz pianists with flawless skills and a big heart. This was a concert to be remembered for a lifetime!

But starting the next day—car troubles. We were driving to Avignon, and the car suddenly flashed a message: *Stop Immediately!* What? We quickly pulled off the highway leading back to Avignon's huge maze-like city center—not a good place to have a car die. What to do? How to find a mechanic on a Sunday in a city we don't know well, and in August (the month when most people go on vacation)? What should have been a relaxing vacation was turning into a stressful nightmare. Luckily there was a small motel at the exit. We pulled into the parking lot, and with the help of the motel owner we secured an appointment with a mechanic for the next day. Remembering our Michel Legrand concert and the joy of that evening helped us remain calm and positive. We got through the next couple days with two different mechanics and several repairs, and finally made it home, sweet home.

ANDORRA

Dan and I took a brief jaunt to Andorra for a quick little getaway. Andorra is a tiny country located high in the Pyrenees and is bordered by Spain and France. It's a three-hour drive from us through beautiful scenery—astounding views of the tall mountains still topped with snow, speckled with spring wildflowers and horses and cows grazing high on the hills. The last hour of the drive is a *looooong* switchback climb uphill. Once over the peak and descending into Andorra, the valley floor is filled with picturesque stone ski lodges and ski lifts dotting the mountains at every turn and makes one think of the fun that could be had on the slopes in wintertime. At over three thousand feet, Andorra la Velle, where we stayed, is the highest capital city in Europe. The official language is Catalan, and it has the ninth highest life expectancy in the world as of 2020: 84–87 years old.

The main reason we went was to see a performance by Cirque du Soleil. Every summer Cirque du Soleil has a month-long residency high in these Pyrenees mountains. This summer's production was called Stellar. We had never seen Cirque de Soleil, and what a mind-blowing experience. The blend of dance, circus, and unbelievable acrobatics transported us to a place of wonder. A giant ship emerged from the clouds, fully rigged and swinging like a pendulum back and forth across the stage. Several performers were riding on the ship, hanging onto the rigging. All of a sudden, a performer jumped off the ship, bounced on a small trampoline below, and literally flew high into the sky, somersaulting back down to his same place on the ship. We were mesmerized watching the acrobats, sometimes in groups of two or three, hurl themselves off the swinging ship and then fly high into the clouds. "Stellar" means "of the stars," and as Cirque du Soleil described: "Dare to fly up into the sky and discover the sensation of being in the clouds!"

MY MIME ADDICTION

I assigned myself a photography project this summer so I would take different pictures than my usual obsession with sunflowers, gargoyles, and other architectural details here in France. My subject was mimes. At many of the music and street festivals, there are fabulously costumed mimes who change their pose as you drop a coin in their box. I find them fascinating and fun to photograph. The most well-known French mime artist was Marcel Marceau, whose performances of his "Bip the Clown" won international

My mime addiction

acclaim. I didn't know this, but Marceau worked for the French Resistance during the World War II. Performing silently as Bip, he kept multiple groups of Jewish children quiet for hours as they escaped over the Alps from occupied France into neutral Switzerland!

The mimes usually stand frozen until you bring forward a coin. In Toulouse central square I watched a fashionably dressed gentleman of the

Another favorite mime

French court stand absolutely still. There was no movement at all except an occasional blink of his eyes. I walked toward him with my euro coin ready to drop in his box, but as I approached he broke his spell and reached out to take it from my hand. Then with a romantic flourish, he kissed my hand and finished with a deep bow. I was caught off guard by this magical moment but my surprise quickly turned into delight. Almost immediately he was right back to his quiet, absolutely still posture.

Another mime I encountered up close and personal in Avignon reached out her hand in invitation to join her on the bright yellow bicycle she was precariously perched on. I sat on the seat as she balanced on the handlebars. As we left Avignon square

I noticed a café where several mimes were getting ready for their performances. Fascinating. It was fascinating to hear their voices, watch them converse, smoke cigarettes, have a beer, put on their white makeup—the real people behind the magic!

THE STRIKE AT THE AVIGNON FESTIVAL

The fifty-year-old Avignon Festival is amazing. Over three hundred theater, dance, and music groups from all over Europe take over the city for three weeks in July. Around every corner there are delightful performance "teasers" to entice you to come see their show that night. The various shows run from morning to night in theaters, churches, wine caves, outdoor grottos, corners of city squares, gardens—everywhere! Tickets are inexpensive except for the main event, which takes place in the courtyard of the Grand Palace of the Popes.

The first year we splurged on a ticket to a main dance event. When we arrived to enter the palace courtyard, there was a strike going on. Actors were parading with placards, but we didn't understand what they were striking against. We entered the theater and were seated. A lone cellist came on stage and began the performance. About forty-five seconds later, it began: loud stamping and clapping from an upper section of the theater. The cellist stopped. Everyone turned around to see. There was a large group of the strikers, over a hundred, all sitting together in one section. They stopped. The cellist began again. Forty-five seconds later the stomping and clapping began even louder. The people in the expensive seats below us stood up and started yelling furiously at the upper-level strikers. Both got louder and louder. We asked the person next to us what was going on. "The theater actors in France are striking for better health care!"

The standoff continued for forty-five minutes. The director of the festival came out to calm things down, asking that the performance be allowed to continue. Nope! Another thirty minutes went by, and finally the gendarme arrived. Soon there was quiet in the theater. The real performance finally started at midnight! We got out about 2:00 a.m. and wandered sleepily back to our little B&B. We didn't find out whether the strike was successful, although France is considered to have one of the best healthcare systems in the world, and we heard of no other strikes that summer. Hopefully they were successful!

LYON, FOODIE HEAVEN

Lyon, a beautiful city—the architecture, the energy, the large parks, the Roman ruins. And the food! It's been named the Gastronomic Capital of France since 1935—over four thousand restaurants for all budgets and twenty-one with Michelin stars! Because of

The Lyon colorful cheeses

its southeastern geographic location, it's a hub for great produce and agricultural delights. Bresse chickens, Charolais beef, the famed pig farms to the west for charcuterie, wine and olive oil from Provence, fish and snails from the marshes close by—these all come to Lyon.

The city is situated between the meeting of the Saone and Rhone Rivers and has been a main transportation route between Northern and Southern Europe since Roman times. Lyon was established as a Roman city in 43 BC and within the first fifty years became the administrative center for Roman Gaul. In World War II, it was heralded as the city of resistance to the Nazis.

We stayed in a small friendly hotel on the Presqu'ile, which is the heart of Lyon. *Presqu'ile* means "peninsula," and it extends from the Vieux Lyon to the north, down to where the Saone and Rhone Rivers converge at the southern tip. It has lots of cafés, shops, restaurants, museums, and large plazas and parks. It's a small peninsula, easily walkable from side to side and end to end—which we did!

There are two wonderful Vieux Lyons (Old Towns). Le Croix-Rousse Old Town on the north side was the center of the silk industry in the sixteenth to eighteenth centuries. By the eighteenth century, silk production was the main industry of Lyon: 28,000 people were registered as silk workers in 1788. This area is known for the *traboules*, hidden covered passageways used by silk merchants to carry silk and supplies between the workshops while being sheltered from the rain. You can find these maze-like, winding traboules marked on the streets and can walk through them even today.

Up the hill, on the western side, is the two-thousand-year-old Roman area with two amphitheaters: the large ancient theater of Fourvière (which has an annual program of music, dance, and theater events) and the smaller theater of Odéon a stone's throw away. Below it and along the Saone River is the other Vieux Lyon—Quartier Saint-Jean, which its colorful cobblestoned streets filled with small cafés, bakeries, restaurants, and modern silk artisans and their ateliers.

One of the first things we did on arrival was go to the Sunday outdoor food market. Artistic piles of fresh veggies were everywhere on the long market street. I had never seen endive on the stalk! Among the many cheese booths, there was a unique booth with red, green, and tourquoise cheese! The green cheese pictured is a Gouda with basil. This beautiful market and also the Paul Bocuse Food Hall close by are the main places where chefs shop. There are a series of large remarkable black-and-white photos throughout the Paul Bocuse Hall that chronicle the great chefs that have apprenticed here in Lyon—including Paul Bocuse himself—and gone on to make their mark on French cuisine.

So many possibilities in Lyon—it's worth several return trips. The Textile and Decorative Arts Museum is a feast for the eyes; the new Musée des Confluences deserves a whole day. At night check out the late-night jazz club La Clef de Voute, with the atmosphere of *les caveaux du jazz* of the Latin Quarter in Paris. And for a great food and history tour, book one of the Lyon food tours. It's worth every euro.

VAN GOGH'S ARLES

Arles is in the Provence region of southern France. This beautiful small city inspired many of Van Gogh's paintings. He lived in Arles from 1888–1889 and created over three hundred paintings and drawings during his short time there. *The Night Café*, *The Yellow Room*, and *Starry Night Over the Rhône*, among others. The famous café is still there and open for business. Stop by and have a glass of wine or coffee! It still looks almost the same as in his painting.

Arles was a provincial capital of ancient Rome and has incredible remains from that era—the amphitheater, the Roman Theater, and the Barbegal aqueduct and mill. Les Arènes d'Arles (the amphitheater), now hosts plays, concerts, and bullfights. We were lucky to attend a folk festival there celebrating the men, women, and horses, and the old traditional ways of courtship. There was dancing, singing, and much flirting in the old Occitan language. To sit on the same seats that the Romans once sat on was an amazing feeling. The city is filled with museums and galleries, and has hosted an international photography exhibition for the last fifty years called Rencontre d'Arles. If you love ancient history, the Museum of Ancient Arles has an exciting and unique vision of their local archaeology.

I was astounded by the Saturday market—over four hundred and fifty stalls and almost two miles long! Held every Saturday morning on the main boulevard, it has beautiful fruits, vegetables, cheeses, flowers, herbs and spices, meat and fish, honey, fresh olives and olive oil, *saucisson d'Arles*, Camargue rice, prawns, crustaceans, *accras* (fritters) of all kinds, bull meat (used in beef stew), seafood paellas, poultry, regional hams, nougat candy, and a whole street of wonderful clothes and crafts. It's a must see!

FRENCH COOKING CLASSES

I've had the opportunity to take several cooking classes in France. The class at Cooking by the Canal du Midi near Carcassonne was a unique experience. We arrived at a shady canopy of plane trees and drove down a long gravel road through a vineyard. At the end of the road there were a series of buildings that had once been animal barns and were converted into holiday apartments and the cooking school.

Heather and David's teaching kitchen was spotless and a lovely mix of old and modern. White cabinets and metal appliances blended beautifully with the worn wooden beams of the barn high above us. There were six of us, and we began with coffee, Heather's homemade croissants, and time to chat about the class and fortify ourselves. From then on it was work, work, work; cook, cook, cook; fun, fun, fun. We learned how to make a delicious cheese soufflé, duck "lollipops" for our main course, golden melting potatoes, a carrot flan, and a gorgeous ginger and nectarine tart with homemade raspberry sorbet for dessert, with berries from their garden. We finished cooking at about one o'clock and carried everything (and lots of wine) out to a table set up right beside the gentle flowing Canal du Midi. A festive feast was enjoyed by us chefs as people in boats riding by on the canal waved to us with a jaunty, *"Bon appetit!"*

Another unique cooking experience was with my friend Suzie, who is a real chef. She and her husband own a B&B about half an hour from us. She offers a small cooking class for four. When I heard this, I quickly corralled my friends Roger, Allan, and Cheryl to take the class too. We arrived at their beautiful B&B to fresh hot coffee and breakfast treats. Suzie had sent us a list of dishes ahead of time to choose three favorites. We chose stuffed mussels, a Greek phyllo tart with chicken and pistachios, and coconut fish curry. The best part about her classes is you bring your own pans, make the whole dish, bake it, and then carry it home to have for dinner that night or freeze it. On top of that, Suzie prepares a yummy lunch (we can have those recipes also) for us all to enjoy together. I really like this format of learning and cooking and going home with three divine ready-made meals.

DAN'S SPEEDO ADVENTURE

One hot summer we drove to Pertuis, close to Aix en Provence, to attend their weeklong big band festival. Every night there are two shows featuring newer big bands as well as well-known big bands from all over Europe, the UK, and even America. The festival is dynamite! We decided we would camp to save money and then splurge on delicious meals during the week. Little did we know that the weather would be unbearably hot during the day and would only finally break at about 4:00 a.m. It felt like a five-hundred-degree oven inside and outside the tent. We could only sleep for a couple hours, and by 11:00 a.m. it was already hard to breathe. I didn't know how I was going to make it through the week.

Luckily someone suggested the village community pool. I'm not a big swimmer, but this sounded like something worth checking out. There were three beautiful full-size pools, one for kids, one for adults, and one for serious swimmers and divers. The pools were surrounded by lounge chairs and umbrellas and even a café and bar! All for two euros a day!

We changed into our swimsuits, ready to dip in, cool off, and spend the day reading, drinking, and relaxing. Dan jumped in first, making a rather big splash. He had also taken his glasses off so he could not see that well. All of a sudden I heard the lifeguard yelling, "Monsieur, Monsieur!" It took me a minute to realize she was yelling at Dan to immediately get out of the pool. He was totally unaware of this. I ran over and yelled, "Dan! She's talking to you!"

I assumed he was in trouble for making such a big splash (kind of a cannonball). But no, it was his California-style swimsuit, just your typical baggy swim trunks that end above the knee. Little did we know that only Speedo-style trunks were allowed in the pool. What!? She said he could not swim until he had Speedo trunks, and they were available in the men's locker room from a vending machine (?!) for about ten euros. Dan slinked off to look at the Speedo vending machine. They were just little bundles of fabric—impossible to tell which size to get. Tiny little packets of weird stretchy material.

So, we left the pool and drove to a store that sells everything Auchan. There we found the Speedo of his dreams. Ha! I was nervous—I had never even seen him in a Speedo. Back to the pool. Dan came out of the men's locker room, looking good and excited to get back in the pool, with another cannonball to celebrate his new Speedo!

COLLIOURE AND THE OCTOPUS

Collioure is a charming artist village about two hours southeast, a few miles north of the Spanish border, and right on the Mediterranean Sea. The first time we went we camped in our tiny tent—the campground was within walking distance of the village and right behind of the campsite was the ocean. One of Dan's favorite things to do is swim in the ocean. For me, not so much. More on that in a minute.

Wandering the narrow, arty cobblestone streets of Collioure is an adventure. You can walk down the middle of the street, stretch out both arms, and almost touch the brightly painted buildings on either side. Art galleries and shops line the flower-filled streets. There are lovely restaurants at every turn and places to sit all along the Med to sip wine or coffee and just relax. The Sunday morning market there is well worth a visit. Paella is a specialty of this area, as are the anchovies from Collioure, which are well-known all over France.

But back to the beach. Dan really, really wanted me to go swimming with him in the Med. I put on my bathing suit, and we grabbed towels and started out the back of the campsite to the beach. We were moseying along and shortly came upon a man walking up from the beach. In his 80s I would say, with a balding, sunburned head and large stomach overflowing his Speedo bathing suit, he's carrying a huge creepy, slippery slick octopus!

"Oh my gosh, where did you find this creature!" I asked.

"It was swimming along with me just now in the ocean!" he said.

WHAT! That's it for me. No swimming in the Med.

Dan tried his best to convince me all would be okay. He was disappointed when I said "No way!" I sat in the shallow water where I could see clearly what was all around me and my feet.

LE JARDIN EXTRAORDINAIRE

In a small village about an hour away there is a magical event that happens only for one weekend in late August. All during the year before, a group of artists and gardeners work together to brainstorm unique and whimsical garden art and plant sculptures. Two weeks before the event, they all gather to do the hundreds of plantings. Our friend Vero has been one of the artists for several years. It's hard to find the words to describe this adventure.

We entered a field surrounded by fifteen-foot-tall sunflowers and began a walking tour along a beautiful meandering stream and through magical woods. Every few feet we came upon amazing art/flower/tree/plant installations: fences woven with sticks, herbs, and flowers; a small hut made with grapevines, the leaves dense with clusters of grapes; fields of wildflowers gently moving in the summer breeze. We continued down to the river, which had been landscaped using rocks, bright white stones, plants, and colorful flowers all planted in whimsical arrangements on the banks.

At every turn your eyes are directed to spectacular views on the ground, high in the trees, beside the flowing river, across the water—every place there was a gem to be seen. Floating circular flower arrangements spiral in the flowing river. A grid of

River garden at Le Jardin Extraordinaire

147

forty cubbyholes is carved into the high dried-mud riverbank, each housing an art object. And one of my favorites: three-dimensional faces made of soil where living grasses grow as hair.

After exiting the walking path you enter the huge meadow where you come upon airy bamboo teepees and domes draped with vines of multicolored hanging orange gourds and unusual climbing flowers and vegetables. Take your time to wander

*Living face at
Le Jardin Extraordinaire*

through the wildflower garden with its beautiful colored flowers all marked with their variety. A fence made of apples leads you up a path for an overview of the whole garden. The magic goes on and on.

We continued to the vegetable garden where school children are taught how to grow plants and tend them. There was an exhibition tent explaining the history of the garden and this wonderful annual event. There is also a food booth to get a light meal for pennies, a craft shop, and our dear friend Vero the hatmaker! Please put this on your list!

RECIPES

CHERRY SORBET

Bring to a boil 7 Tbsp. water and ¼ cup sugar until the sugar dissolves to make a simple syrup. Add in ¾ cup whole milk, ½ cup heavy cream, and 1 ½ cups cherries, pits removed and cut into small pieces. Put into your ice cream maker and enjoy!

WHITE BEAN, BLUE CHEESE, AND CHORIZO SALAD

Drain one 15-ounce can of white cannellini beans and put in a bowl. Make dressing: Whisk together 4 Tbsp. olive oil, 2 Tbsp. sherry vinegar, 2 tsp. honey, and 1 tsp. Dijon mustard and season with salt and pepper. Pour the dressing over the beans and toss. Add 2 Tbsp. slivered almonds, 6 chopped cherry tomatoes, slices of chorizo, ham or pepperoni, and ⅓ cup blue cheese crumbles. Toss lightly.

RATATOUILLE CRUMBLE

Preheat oven to 400°F. Cut 3 zucchini and 2 eggplants into rounds and roast in the oven with olive oil, salt, and pepper, 30–40 minutes till veggies are tender and browned. While roasting, chop 3 large tomatoes.

In a skillet with 1 Tbsp. olive oil, sauté 1 chopped red onion, 2 garlic cloves sliced, and 2 tsp. fresh rosemary. Add in the tomatoes and ½ cup pine nuts (I use cashews instead). Cook over medium heat until sauce-like.

In a separate bowl mix ⅓ cup flour, ⅓ cup parmesan, a little salt and pepper, and 1 Tbsp. lemon thyme. Add ¼ cup melted butter and mix till soft crumbs form.

In a casserole dish, layer eggplant, then zucchini, then tomato sauce. Repeat. Top with the parmesan crumble. Bake 20–30 minutes until crumble is golden brown.

Nectarine and Ginger Tart

Preheat oven to 400°F. Buy or make a pastry shell or pie crust and place on a piece of parchment paper in your baking dish. Cut 6 nectarines into slices. Peel and grate a 2-inch piece of fresh ginger. Melt 3 Tbsp. butter and baste the bottom of the pastry with it. Sprinkle ¼ cup brown sugar on top of butter. Layer on the nectarine slices, slightly overlapping. Sprinkle the grated ginger on top. (I sometimes use crystallized ginger instead of fresh). Bake 15–25 minutes till golden brown. Yum!

About the Author

DAYLE DOROSHOW IS A MIXED MEDIA ARTIST who loves fashion, food, and France. She makes large textile wall hangings and unique handmade jewelry, all inspired by her travels and love of ancient history and its artisans. Her biggest dream came true in 2004 when she started teaching art workshops in a small French village in southwest France. After nineteen summers there, she loves sharing the beauty of the people and places in the Lauragais and nurturing the creative spirit in all of us.

www.ingramcontent.com/pod-product-compliance
Lightning Source LLC
Chambersburg PA
CBHW050818090426
42737CB00021B/3425